Understanding Industrial Society

A Sociological Guide

Robin Theobald
Principal Lecturer in Sociology
Faculty of Business, Management
and Social Studies
University of Westminster

St. Martin's Press

First published in Great Britain 1994 by
THE MACMILLAN PRESS LTD
Houndmills, Basingstoke, Hampshire RG21 2XS
and London
Companies and representatives
throughout the world

A catalogue record for this book is available
from the British Library.

ISBN 0–333–48538–6 hardcover
ISBN 0–333–48539–4 paperback

1759814

Printed in Hong Kong

First published in the United States of America 1994 by
Scholarly and Reference Division,
ST. MARTIN'S PRESS, INC.,
175 Fifth Avenue,
New York, N.Y. 10010

ISBN 0–312–12067–2

Library of Congress Cataloging-in-Publication Data applied for

Goe, and catche a falling starre,
Get with child a mandrake roote,
Tell me, where all past yeares are,
Or who cleft the Divels foot,
Teach me to heare Mermaides singing,
Or to keep off envies stinging,
And finde
What winde
Serves to advance an honest minde.

John Donne, *'Song'*

Contents

List of Boxes, Figures and Tables

Preface

The origins of this book lie in more than a decade of teaching the sociology of industrialisation to business studies and other non-social science students. This experience has persuaded me that there is still room for another introductory text in sociology. I emphasise 'text' as this is not a textbook as such. Rather its aim is to introduce the reader to a sociological perspective on the emergence and continuing development of industrial capitalist societies. The book assumes that there is a body of students, mainly outside the social sciences, who seek a general understanding of the major social consequences of long-term economic change. Since it also assumes that most of its readers will end up working in management, the book eventually focuses upon the business enterprise and social relations within it. However, this is emphatically not a text in the sociology of organisations, many excellent examples of which already exist. Rather this book aims to provide a general background which will lay the foundations for subsequent and more detailed study of organisational processes and problems of management.

On the basis of experience in a number of institutions and courses I feel it reasonable to take the view that the overwhelming majority of readers of this book will come to it with minimal knowledge of the social sciences. For this reason I have consciously sought to avoid becoming involved in the conceptual and theoretical debates which most sociology textbooks consider obligatory. Whilst core social science students may find such controversies both necessary and absorbing, non-specialists can often be put off by the apparent complexity of the issues and what is perceived, rightly or wrongly, as the obscurity of the terminology. This I feel is a great pity as I am absolutely convinced that the discipline of sociology offers numerous useful insights into the manifold ways in which social forces and the outworkings of social change affect our daily lives. Accordingly I here limit myself to introducing a number of key themes and issues striving to point up their relevance to an understanding of modern society and its development. In indicating these themes and issues I am hoping that at least some of the readership may be stimulated to pursue them further in the more specialist literature. With regard to those who are not so stimulated I entertain the modest ambition that when they close this book they will have a greater understanding of industrial society and the process of industrialisation than when they first opened it.

It will soon be apparent to those who venture to read what follows that the underlying approach here is clearly influenced by a developmental perspective. This, in many respects, is dictated by the basic theme, industrial society, which in necessarily evoking comparisons with pre- and post-industrial counterparts is difficult to treat other than developmentally. But it also reflects my own teaching and research experience in the area of development studies and in particular the *global* orientation of development literature. The concept of a world capitalist system through whose arteries all societies, from the most developed to the most peripheral, are interlinked, I have found particularly useful and insightful. Thus I subscribe strongly to the view that no single society can be adequately understood unless situated within the overall context of the basic shifts and phases of growth and contraction of this world system. Accordingly, after a brief introductory chapter which discusses the relevance of sociology to business, I move in Chapter 2 to look at the emergence of a *world* economy and at its current principal characteristics. Chapter 3 aims to identify the essentials of industrialism and capitalism by comparing them to their pre-industrial pre-capitalist counterparts. Chapter 4 seeks to emphasise the continuous nature of the process of industrialisation by pointing up the profound social and economic differences between nineteenth- and twentieth-century capitalism. Chapter 5 focuses upon the firm itself and the consequences of industrial concentration for formal organisation as well as for the functions and basic characteristics of management. Chapter 6 examines the development of management in the sense of a 'science' dedicated to the goal of the efficient organisation of work. Chapter 7 concerns itself with the negative consequences of the diffusion of mass-production techniques whilst Chapter 8 returns to the theme of continuing change with a critical look at the notion of a post-industrial society. Finally, in a brief concluding chapter I make a few tentative observations about the future course of global development.

In writing this book I owe an incalculable debt to my wife, Elizabeth, and three sons, Wally, Ernie and Dave, for their exemplary forbearance in the face of (I regret) ever more frequent bouts of ranting. I must also thank my University of Westminster colleague, Bob Freedman, for teaching me a great deal about history and rhyming slang; Anne Poole for the characteristically perceptive aside that prompted me to rewrite much of this book; and, of course, Cas Spencer for her invaluable help in the preparation of the manuscript. Last but by no means least, I want to express my gratitude to Professor Aurelio Rigoli and the staff and associates of the Centro Internazionale di Etnostoria, Palermo, not only for awarding me one of the Pitre-Salomone Marino prizes in 1990, but for the warmth and hospitality shown to me during my visit to Palermo in 1992. Having acknowledged these debts I must stress that the responsibility for what follows is entirely my own.

ROBIN THEOBALD

1 Business and Society

It is obvious that all societies, from simple hunting bands to the complex industrial societies in which we live, must produce the basic goods and services their members depend upon. All societies, that is, have an economy in the sense of mechanisms which permit the production and circulation of goods and services. However, the principles which underpin these processes of production and circulation vary from society to society. In most pre-industrial societies kinship is one of the most important mechanisms or 'institutions' through which goods and services are allocated. That is to say, one gains access to food, shelter and personal security primarily as a member of a particular family group. In our type of society, the family is by no means redundant as a provider of important goods and services, from cooked meals and washed clothes to an overall feeling of security. Nonetheless we obtain a large proportion of what we need – food, clothes, consumer durables – by paying for them with money. Monetary transactions are the predominant feature of our type of 'capitalist' society and when we talk about 'business' we think primarily in terms of money-making. A successful business person is someone who makes a lot of money for him/herself and/or high profits for his/her company. Money, in fact, operates at three levels in relation to the firm. First, we invest money or 'capital' in a particular project, whether it is to buy machinery for making furniture or a computer to provide financial services. A business person will, second, pay out wages to buy the labour, whether intellectual or manual, of employees. And last, by selling the goods and services on the open market the entrepreneur hopes to make a profit. Capital, wages, markets and profits thus seem to be the basic ingredients of 'business' in our type of society.

The question of the precise nature of capitalism we shall return to in Chapter 3. For the time being let us think a little more about this difficult term 'society'. What does it mean when we talk about the 'society in which we live', for example?

For a start it seems that society has some kind of existence apart from ourselves. This existence manifests itself in our relationship with others. Throughout our lives we are drawn into a series of relationships with family and friends, at school, college, work, leisure and so on. Furthermore, the people with whom we interact in these various contexts have certain expectations as to what we should do and how we should behave, just as we have of them. So at work, for example, we are not only expected to

1

perform effectively and competently the tasks for which we have been appointed, but also to 'get on' with the individuals and groups with whom we come into contact in that context. If we do not meet, in a general sense, their expectations, if we do not 'fit in' or are seen as unreliable, rude, offhand, aggressive, uncooperative, devious or whatever, we are likely to encounter censure, hostility, ridicule, contempt, withdrawal of cooperation, avoidance, and perhaps dismissal. Now all of us some of the time do not meet the expectations that others have of us. Sometimes we are uncooperative, bad-tempered, aggressive, do not do what we are supposed to in what is considered to be the right kind of humour. But those of us who consistently and repeatedly break with social conventions run the risk of being labelled as 'odd', 'untrustworthy', a 'troublemaker' or 'anti-social', and may be shunned, isolated or perhaps even incarcerated in an institution. The fact is that most of us conform most of the time primarily because we are dependent upon society. That is to say, we are dependent upon our social relationships with others to meet our fundamental needs: our physical needs for food, warmth, shelter, security, sexual gratification; and, just as important, our psychic needs for esteem and love. This dependence means that these relationships exercise considerable sway over us. These relationships may be termed 'social structure'. Social structure expresses itself in such social institutions as the family, school, college and work. By institutions here we do not mean, in the first instance, buildings, bricks and mortar, in the sense of an educational or penal institution. The term institution in a sociological sense, signifies patterns of behaviour which have been established over time. Take the family for example: we are born into a family situation which preexists us and in relation to which there are ideas and expectations about how fathers and mothers, sisters and brothers, grandparents and grandchildren should behave towards one another. These expectations are not fixed but change over time. Fifty years ago single-parent families were unusual and were generally regarded as shameful. Fifty years ago fathers played a much smaller role in childcare than they do today. Despite these changes the patterns and expectations which they express have or had some kind of independent existence. This independent existence is embodied in a society's *culture* – a collection of ideas, attitudes, norms, beliefs and values which is transmitted to successive generations via social institutions. We can thus say that society consists of three basic elements: individuals, culture and structure.

We as individuals are born into a family situation which not only cares for us but initiates us into our society and its way of doing things. This is a process which is termed *socialisation* and which involves us in playing a succession of *social roles*: son, daughter, brother, sister, niece, nephew,

Box 1.1   The basic elements of society

Culture	Social institutions	Individuals
Norms	Family	
Values	School	
Beliefs	Work	
Attitudes	Mass media	
Ways of behaving	Government	
Ways of doing things	Religion	

friend, pupil, student, part-time employee at the local supermarket, trainee accountant, father, mother and so on. Each role has built into it a set of expectations about how it should be performed. Socialisation is usually divided into primary and secondary stages. Primary socialisation refers to the crucial early stages during infancy which take place in the intimate atmosphere of the immediate family and during which the basic contours of personality are formed. Secondary socialisation begins roughly when we have acquired a conception of who we are, that is, a conception of *self*. The onset of secondary socialisation is usually associated with the acquisition of a reasonable competence in language since it is only through language that we are able to develop a conception of ourselves, the 'I', as opposed to other people, the 'other'. Secondary socialisation goes on throughout our lives as we continue to adopt new roles, ultimately that of the dying.

Turning from society in general to our focus in this book, the business enterprise, it may be apparent that the firm too is a kind of mini-society. It has its own organisational structure, a set of (usually hierarchical) positions, from managing director to canteen assistant, each position having its own specific duties and responsibilities. The firm will also have its specific culture in the sense of an accumulated set of values, beliefs and norms relating to how it as a firm behaves in relation both to the external environment and to employees. But employees are not, of course, robots who slot passively into their organisational roles. They bring with them expectations, ambitions, needs, prejudices, frustrations and so forth. These attributes will be a function of their cumulative social experiences in the family, school, college, other organisations and in the wider society generally. In other words all business organisations exist in and must come to terms with the environment in which they operate. This is obvious in the case of the economic environment as clearly any firm must adapt to its market as well as take account of such factors as interest rates, the rate of inflation, capital and labour costs, exchange rates and movements within the international economy.

Figure 1.1   The business firm and its environment

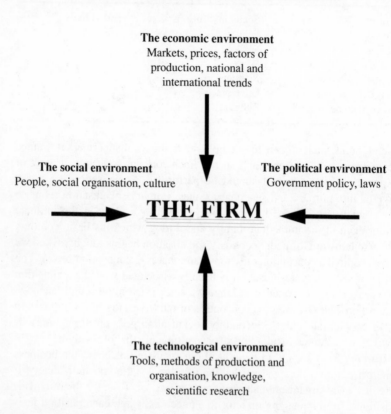

The economic environment
Markets, prices, factors of
production, national and
international trends

The social environment
People, social organisation, culture

The political environment
Government policy, laws

THE FIRM

The technological environment
Tools, methods of production and
organisation, knowledge,
scientific research

In addition to the economic dimension the firm must come to terms with politics and the activities of government whether national or local. In the first instance business activities will be affected by general policy decisions relating, say, to taxation, interest rates, rates of inflation and unemployment. But in addition to these, firms will also need to concern themselves with decisions relating to such areas as health and safety, product standards and environmental pollution as well as the general area of company law, finance and accounting. For these reasons business people frequently seek to influence government policy decisions usually through representative associations such as chambers of commerce or the Confederation of British Industry.

Clearly the operation of any business enterprise is powerfully affected by the technological environment. Technology consists, first, of knowledge

– the state and level of development of scientific knowledge that exists in a given society – and second, of the way in which this knowledge manifests itself in tools and machines, by which we refer to a vast range of artefacts, from mechanical drills to computer-operated milling machines, from filing cabinets to microprocessors. But we should also remember, third, that technology manifests itself in the actual organisation of work: the assignment of tasks, the coordination of separate activities, monitoring and control systems, as well as the procedures for taking decisions and implementing policy.

Fourth, the firm must come to terms with its social environment. In the real world this social dimension is not separate from the other three, all of them interrelating and influencing each other. Governments take decisions about supporting or not supporting scientific research or the development of particular technologies. Individual groups and classes may band together in order to seek to influence government policy over, say, the environment or the level of unemployment. However, for analytical purposes it is helpful to treat the social dimension separately.

That aspect of society which most obviously impinges upon the operations of the firm is the size and character of a country's population. If you are opening a restaurant or a clothes shop in a given town you would need to have some idea about whether it contains enough people to produce sufficient demand for the meals you cook or the clothes you sell. But this is not just a question of numbers. You would also want to know something about the character of the population – the age distribution for example, the proportion under 21 or over 60 and, furthermore, the manner in which these proportions are likely to change over the next decade. If you open your restaurant or shop in an area which is heavily based on a declining industry you may find that in five to ten years a large slice of your custom has disappeared as those of working age move away to seek employment elsewhere.

In relation to the character of populations much has been written about different patterns of consumption between classes. We are familiar with terms such as 'up-market' and 'down-market', terms which, whatever we think of them, suggest that different social groups tend to have different tastes in clothes, holidays, cars or whatever, and that businesses need to be aware of these differences. For example, so-called quality newspapers advertise different products from their tabloid counterparts because market research has shown that the qualities are bought by different social categories with different tastes. The essential point is that assumptions about diverse social categories with varying patterns of consumption make sound economic sense.

This is not of course to argue that every entrepreneur has to make a detailed study of the demographic characteristics of his/her market. For those who cannot afford expensive market research inspired guesswork must suffice. The point is, however, that in this age of intense competition if he/she is only mildly wrong the economic consequences are likely to be disastrous.

The second aspect of society which affects business activities is social organisation. The most obvious example of this is organisation of the educational system. Firms require personnel with the appropriate background and training. Are schools, colleges and universities producing enough manpower with the requisite skills and orientations? Whether they are or not will be a consequence not simply of the government's educational policy, but of a whole confection of career decisions, attitudes and aspirations which will themselves be a reflection of social organisation and culture. Culture we shall come onto shortly; let us in the meantime look at two more brief examples of the way in which social organisation – in this case the family – affects business. The first concerns the survival of the extended family among certain ethnic minorities. The point is that this type of family and the strong solidarity it expresses may be particularly suited to the operation of certain types of business which require very long hours for low economic returns, that is, where profits are too low to permit the payment of conventional wage rates. The second example comes from a study which looked at a number of firms in the north of England. In some of these firms young female employees seemed unresponsive to monetary incentives, apparently being content to take home the same basic amount every week. After close investigation it was found that the standard family practice in this area was for the young women to hand over their wage packet unopened to their mothers who gave them back a fixed amount of pocket money. Had they earned more through overtime or piece-work they would still have received only the basic, fixed amount, hence the ineffectiveness of material inducements.

Admittedly this last example, in that it is dealing with custom, hovers between social organisation and culture. In reality the two are necessarily closely interrelated. Nonetheless, for the purposes of understanding, it is worth highlighting culture once more in the specific context of business. It will be apparent that the general complex of values and attitudes which make up the general culture in a society will have something specific to say about business and work. It is widely believed, for example, that the Japanese love to work whereas Europeans, particularly the British, are thought to be much less enthusiastic about the eight hours they spend in the factory or office. Whether such perceptions are entirely accurate is highly debatable. The point is that since they are fairly firmly embedded in popular and especially management thinking, they affect our behaviour and policies. As we shall see in a subsequent chapter the Japanese approach to management and to the organisation of work generally is currently embraced by many management gurus as the solution to Britain's economic ills. The general point is that conceptions of 'work', 'success', 'pulling one's weight', 'teamwork', 'the good of the country', 'the good of the company', through a complex process of refraction, will be diffused through numerous groups and classes in society. Clearly the influence of such conceptions will vary between different groups of workers and managers. One of the tasks for the sociologist is to describe and account for such variations. In doing this he/she will attempt to base such conclusions that are reached on sound evidence that has been collected in as systematic a way as possible. That is to say, he/she will attempt to be as scientific as possible, hence sociology is included amongst the social sciences. But is it a science?

Certainly early sociologists such as the alleged founder Auguste Comte (1798–1857) believed that the new discipline could be as scientific as the natural sciences. Studying society or social phenomena for Comte was basically no different from studying molecules, biological organisms or chemical elements. However, most contemporary sociologists would not now take such a position, conceding that human behaviour is much more complex than most of the phenomena studied by natural scientists. This is not least because human beings, having the facility of language, are able to think and reflect upon their own behaviour. However, whilst sociology is not a science in the strict sense of the term, it would be generally agreed that, in so far as it is possible, the principal methods of the sciences should inform sociological study. Basically this means that the theories developed by sociologists and the general statements that they make should, first, be firmly grounded in *empirical* evidence, that is, evidence from the real world, and, second, that this evidence or data should be collected in a systematic fashion in order to form as representative a view as possible of the area of study.

Probably the most obvious way of acquiring data systematically is through the administration of a standard questionnaire to all respondents (the subjects of one's investigation), or, if this number is too large, to a random sample. However it may be that standardised questionnaires are unsuited to the kind of data we seek, or to the social context into which we are researching. Questionnaires are useful for collecting reasonably unequivocal information such as age, education, income, social class background, occupation, as well as fairly uncomplicated responses to statements of the 'agree – strongly agree – disagree – strongly disagree' variety.

Where we wish to explore attitudes and perceptions more deeply it is likely that other methods such as loosely structured interviews would be more appropriate. Alternatively the sociological investigator may spend some time participating in a social activity over a given period, perhaps even living with a particular group or community. The method of 'participant observation' has been used with considerable success by social anthropologists in the study of small-scale tribal societies and village communities. But participant observation has also been used effectively by sociologists particularly in relation to areas of behaviour where the use of questionnaires might be too obtrusive: informal groups at work, delinquent gangs and other deviant groups, and religious movements. The idea is that by spending some considerable time with the group he/she is studying the sociologist is, to a degree, absorbed into its activities, becomes less of an intruder and is therefore able to build up a more realistic and comprehensive picture of this aspect of social behaviour.

In many research contexts it is likely that some combination of these and other methods – the study of documents or written biographies for example – is desirable. But whatever methods are used the reasons for choosing them should be clearly stated along with the other assumptions that underly our research. The idea is that every aspect of our research should be 'open', that is to say, open to critical scrutiny by other sociologists or anyone who is interested.

Sociological research then strives to 'get close' to social reality. Nonetheless we will never arrive at the 'truth' primarily because the bulk of the information we use comes from individuals who are participants in our field of study and are therefore 'involved' in a variety of ways in the social relationships which comprise it. Equally important the researcher will never be able to exclude entirely his/her own preconceptions, value judgements, opinions and prejudices. However, through the cautious and painstaking assembly of data the sociologist aims to make reasoned observations and generalisations about human behaviour. The sociologist tries especially to avoid and, if possible, counter, the shallow impressionistic sweeping statements, the instant black and white diagnoses with which we are daily bombarded by politicians, TV pundits, investigating journalists; the 'experts' through whom is filtered the social reality that lies beyond our immediate sphere of relationships.

We may therefore say that sociology is the systematic study of society. However since society is both stable and constantly changing we might accurately define it as the 'systematic study of social order and social change'. Change in fact is the major theme of this book, its fundamental point being that the society in which we live is subject to permanent change, change now so radical that it is no exaggeration to claim that the world this author was brought up in was utterly different from that which exists now. In order therefore to understand our society and particularly to gain some insight as to where it may be going, we need to have some knowledge of its origins and the stages through which it has passed. Accordingly the next two chapters have a somewhat historical slant, Chapter 2 dealing with the emergence of a global economy and Chapter 3 looking at the origins of industrialism and capitalism.

BIBLIOGRAPHY

Brown, D. and Harrison, M. J. (1978) *A Sociology of Industrialisation* (London: Macmillan).
Wood, D. J. (1990) *Business and Society* (London: HarperCollins).

2 One World, One Economy

Whether we are aware of it or not the international economy permeates our everyday lives. A good deal of the food and drink we consume, although no doubt processed here, comes from outside the United Kingdom, whether rice from the United States or Surinam, oranges from Spain or Israel, cocoa and pineapples from the Ivory Coast, coffee from Kenya or cauliflowers and potatoes from Brittany. The shirts and dresses we wear are increasingly likely to have been made in India or Hong Kong, our shoes in Italy or Brazil, our hi-fi, TV or video in Japan or Singapore. Whether the car we drive comes from Japan, France or Germany, the iron ore from which its steel body is made probably originates in Australia, Canada or Brazil, the copper in the electrics from Chile or Zambia, chrome on the bumper bars from South Africa, Thailand or Turkey. The price of the petrol we put in its tank is heavily determined by decisions made in Riyadh, Jakarta, Algiers or Tehran. If we have a mortgage, the interest rate we pay is strongly influenced by the budget deficit the United States government chooses to run, as will be the interest on the overdraft our small business has with the bank. If we export, the price of the commodity we manufacture will be much affected by the exchange value of the pound against other currencies, this value being the outcome of a whole series of complex international movements and pressures.

Yet this all-pervasive international economy is, in the perspective of human evolution, a relatively recent development. With our Eurocentric view of the world it is worth recalling that northern Europe five hundred years ago stood on the periphery of a world overshadowed by the Ming imperial dynasty of China, the most powerful and advanced civilisation of that era. In the West the focus of economic and cultural activity was the Mediterranean where the Italian city-states were linked commercially with the Near East and North Africa. Three centuries later the once backward northern Europe, and Britain particularly, had become economically so powerful as to pull vast areas of the world into its orbit.

Why Britain and Europe and not Ming China became the 'workshop of the world' cannot be our concern here. Our main purpose is to understand the process of industrialisation, especially its socioeconomic consequences. It is therefore essential to look briefly at the emergence and character of this global economy, not only because its expansion was a vital prerequisite for industrialisation, but also because movements and shifts within it continue crucially to affect the development path taken by Britain.

THE EMERGENCE OF A WORLD ECONOMY

> In fourteen hundred and ninety-two
> Columbus sailed the ocean blue.

This rather banal couplet which many of us may have chanted at junior school marks a period which was of fundamental importance for subsequent world development. Columbus's discovery of America was one of numerous voyages of discovery west to the New World and east to Asia and beyond which took place at the end of the fifteenth and throughout the sixteenth centuries. The primary motive behind these extremely hazardous journeys was the quest for economic wealth, either the luxury items of long-distance trade – spices, silks, precious stones, porcelain; or precious metals – gold and silver – to pay for these commodities. The subjugation of the Near East and many parts of southern Europe by the Ottoman Turks in the fifteenth century was a major factor behind the search by the Portuguese for an alternative route round the coast of Africa to Asia. At the end of the fifteenth century Portuguese possessions outside Europe included several island groups in the Atlantic, the Gulf of Guinea and a few trading stations on the coast of West Africa. At these trading posts cloth and hardware were bartered for slaves and gold-dust. After Vasco da Gama discovered the sea route to India in 1598 the Portuguese extended their trading ventures to the east coast of Africa, the northern shores of the Indian Ocean and the Malay archipelago, their aim being to gain control over the lucrative spice trade with the East. During this period spices were needed in Europe not only as condiments but also as preservatives, especially of meat. In fact the Portuguese never secured a monopoly over the trade, having to share it with Arab, Persian and Indian merchants although not, for nearly a century, with other Europeans.

Whereas the Portuguese struck east, at least initially, their Spanish neighbours pushed west across the Atlantic, driven primarily, as Adam Smith was to observe, by 'the thirst for gold' (*The Wealth of Nations*). Spanish settlement on the Latin American mainland began in 1509, focusing on Mexico and Peru not only because, being densely populated, they provided labour for the conquerors, but also because of their productive silver mines. By the 1560s silver had become the chief export to Spain with cochineal (used for dyeing), tallow (for candles and soap) and sugar a long way behind. The growing interpendence of an emerging world economy is apparent even at this stage in the transshipment of silver from the New World to the Philippines, by the end of the 1560s also a Spanish possession, where it was used for the purchase of Chinese silk. Some of this silk was bought by an expanding Spanish aristocracy in Mexico, some reexported to Peru and some even shipped back across the Atlantic to Spain.

By the middle of the sixteenth century the Portuguese had established themselves in the New World, setting up slave plantations in Brazil. Between 1575 and 1600 Brazil became the foremost sugar-producing area in the western world. By the end of the sixteenth century Portugal and Spain, now united under a single monarchy, dominated the three principal empires of world trade: the silver empire of Spanish America, the spice empire of Asia and the sugar empire of the South Atlantic.

The early seventeenth century marks the growing incursion of northern Europeans into these three trading spheres. Both in the Indies and the New World the Dutch and the British began to force their way into the Iberian empire. In the 1630s the Dutch West India Company launched a powerful offensive against Spanish shipping in the Caribbean, severely disrupting the flow of silver to Spain. Seizing the opportunities provided by an overall situation of military adventurism, English settlers were able to establish themselves on some of the smaller islands of the Caribbean. By the second half of the seventeenth century islands such as Antigua, Anguilla, Barbados and Grenada housed prosperous sugar plantations employing African slave labour. African labour was needed because the indigenous population of these islands and those parts of the Latin American mainland where a plantation economy was set up had been drastically reduced or in many cases exterminated by conquest and disease. The transatlantic slave trade, remnants of which survived until the end of the nineteenth century, was at the centre of a rapidly developing international economy. Through an endless series of economic transactions Europe, Asia, Africa and the Americas were interlinked. European planters in the Caribbean and parts of Brazil produced mainly sugar but also cocoa, rice and tobacco for export to Europe. The increased demand for sugar in Europe is partly associated with the rising consumption there of tea which, in turn, was imported from China. The plantation owners were supplied with food by the small farmers of North America, again European settlers, as well as by the Newfoundland fisheries. The bills of exchange which the North American farmers got from the sale of their food, and the plantation owners for the sale of their sugar, could be used to purchase manufactures from Europe. The slaves who worked the plantations were bought in West Africa from African dealers in exchange for cotton cloth (much of it from India) and commodities manufactured in Europe, such as hardware and firearms. The link between slaving and manufacturing is particularly apparent in the case of Liverpool which by the beginning of the eighteenth century had become a major commercial centre in the 'triangular trade'. (Manufactured goods to West Africa, slaves to the Americas, sugar, cotton, tobacco back to Europe represent the three sides of the triangle.) Liverpool slavers could not only obtain their supplies of manufactured goods from the Lancashire hinterland but Manchester businessmen also granted them the credit facilities which were vital for their long-distance trade.

The link between the slave trade and the expansion of English manufacturing is a controversial one. It has led some historians to argue that industrialisation was made possible only by the large-scale enslavement of the black man. In Marxist terminology the triangular trade permitted the 'primitive accumulation' of capital without which the Industrial Revolution could not have taken off. It is not possible for us to legislate on this question in this book. Suffice it to say that most historians would agree that the slave trade and the profits from it made some contribution to the industrialisation of Britain. More important is the broader context: the overall expansion of trade required the shipping of bulky items over long distances, the provision of long-term credit facilities, the financing of large stocks and large-scale capital investments. In short the organisation of trade on this scale and over these distances necessitated what amounted to a *commercial* revolution and without this commercial revolution the Industrial Revolution could not have taken place.

A good deal more will be said about the Industrial Revolution in the next chapter. For the time being we simply note that the term refers to the transition from a predominantly agricultural to a predominantly industrial economy, that is, an economy in which inanimate sources of power are harnessed to the production of material goods. Until the end of the eighteenth century the motive power behind production was primarily human or animal muscle. Wind and water were also used but their supply was unpredictable. The invention of the steam engine and rotary transmission enables power not only to be applied in much larger amounts than before but with much greater regularity and reliability. Many machines could be gathered in one place and operated simultaneously from a single source of power. The new techniques made possible massive rises in output: in 1780 Britain's output of iron was smaller than that of France; by 1848 it was greater than that of the rest of the world. By then Britain's coal production represented two-thirds and cotton cloth one-half of total world output.

THE DIFFUSION OF INDUSTRIALISM

For the first half of the nineteenth century Britain remained the world's leading manufacturer and the world's only industrial society. In the second half of the nineteenth century, however, the industrial system was diffused to other parts of Europe and across the Atlantic to the United States. By then, of course, the process of industrialisation had been rumbling on for over half a century so that the character of the industrial system differed quite markedly from what had existed in 1800. In fact between 1870 and 1914 there took place what amounted to a second industrial revolution. Whereas the early stages of the revolution had been dominated by coal, iron and cotton, in this second stage steel-making and chemical production came to the fore with electricity and subsequently the internal combustion engine increasingly used as sources of power. Again, whereas Britain took the lead in the early stages, the initiative now passed to the Germans and the Americans. On the eve of the Second World War Britain had been over-taken in many areas by her two major competitors. Britain pioneered the chemical industry and the invention of aniline dyes but by 1913 Britain accounted for only 11 per cent of world output as against 24 per cent for Germany and 34 per cent for the USA. Although the Bessemer convertor which made the mass production of steel possible was developed in Britain, British industry was slow to adopt it for commercial purposes. Accordingly British steel production fell behind that of Germany and the USA. By 1910 the USA was producing twice as much basic steel alone than the total steel production of Britain. Similarly the output of the British electrical industry by 1913 was little more than a third of that of its German counterpart. The invention and development of the internal combustion engine, the diesel, the electric dynamo and electric traction largely took place in Germany. The sewing-machine, the typewriter, the filament lamp and the telephone were invented in the USA.

But whilst falling behind her major rivals in terms of industrial production, in one area, finance capital, Britain easily retained her dominance. In addition to being the 'workshop of the world' Britain was also its 'clearing-house', its banker, shipper, insurer and above all its chief investor. With nearly £4000m in overseas assets in 1914 Britain enjoyed a commanding lead over the rest of the field. At this time the *total* foreign investment of France, Germany, Belgium, Holland and the USA amounted to less than £5500m. The importance of the 'invisible' earnings from *finance capital* cannot be overstated. For example, between 1865 and 1913 Britain's trade deficit grew from £58.2m to £134.3m. However, during the same period the overall balance of payments moved from a surplus of £21.8m to

£187.9m. The growing deficit on trade, in other words, was transformed into an expanding surplus because of the rapidly increasing contribution of the commercial activities of the 'City'.

Between 1870 and 1914 the world economy knitted together in a way that had previously been inconceivable. This knitting together was made possible by the revolution in communications, with railways and shipping taking the main share but with canals, river navigation and roads also playing a significant role. Now that goods could be moved rapidly and cheaply over the earth's surface it became economical for Europe to draw more of its food and raw materials over vast distances. After 1850 supplies of wheat came increasingly from Australia, the American Mid-West, Canada, Argentina and India. The development of refrigeration and canning techniques in the 1880s made it profitable to raise vast herds of cattle in Argentina and Texas for consumption in Europe. By the end of the nineteenth century Britain was dependent on overseas supplies for four-fifths of its wheat and two-fifths of its meat.

Whilst examining the diffusion of industrialism it is crucial to be aware that the economic conditions under which the process unfolded varied very considerably between countries. This is particularly the case in relation to the level of state involvement in the respective economies. What is all too often treated as the model route to industrialisation – that taken by Britain – entailed minimal levels of state intervention in conformity with *laissez-faire* (free-market) thinking. In fact the first fifty years of the nineteenth century saw the progressive dismantling in Britain of a range of fiscal and economic barriers to trade and the mobility of labour. From 1820 tariffs were reduced, the Navigation Laws liberalised and eventually abolished, and the Corn Laws abolished, as well as remaining protectionist legislation. Generally speaking, the half-century from 1820 to 1870 in Britain, Europe and the United States is one which saw an overall reduction of restraints on trade such as tariffs, customs, dues and monopolies. It is the classic example of *laissez-faire* expansion. After 1870 not only does this trend go into reverse but so far as continental Europe is concerned the state takes a much more pro-active role in the economy. What precisely did the state do? We may identify four major categories of activity.

First, the state can actively restructure the institutions of society in order to create an environment that is favourable to the development of capitalism. If a country is fragmented into a significant number of semi-autonomous provinces or principalities each with its own systems of law, weights and measures and even currencies, then such conditions obviously pose serious impediments to the expansion of trade and commerce. To varying degrees such conditions did exist in pre-revolutionary France, in

Italy before 1861 and in Germany in 1871. In fact before these dates neither a 'Germany' nor an 'Italy' could be said to exist in the sense of nation-states. Accordingly in both cases the state played a major role in fostering political unification and, along with revolutionary France, in promoting the standardisation of weights and measures, currency and law, as well as the abolition of internal tariffs.

Second, government may provide services which can be geared to the needs of the industrial system. The direct promotion of scientific research and technical education is an obvious example. Here it may be noted that the promotion of technical education generally began much earlier on the Continent than it did in Britain. Germany, for example, not only took a lead in this respect, but in addition, and like France, set up an official information service which sent experts to Britain and the United States to bring back and disseminate technical information.

Third, the state can manipulate taxes, subsidies or markets in such a way as to stimulate private enterprise. It can protect specific firms or industries through the imposition of tariffs on incoming products in the same areas. In the second half of the nineteenth century we note a growing clamour amongst European agricultural interests for government protection of their products, mainly against imports of cheap American grain. In Germany, where tariffs on most imports had been abolished by 1877, complaints by agricultural producers about cheap American wheat and by iron and steel producers about declining prices led to the readoption of protectionist measures. France soon followed Germany's example with agriculture leading the field. Other countries followed suit, leading to a series of tariff wars in Europe. But in addition to protecting agriculture or infant industries from external competition, governments might favour developing industries by subsidising them through the award of government contracts on very generous terms, by guaranteeing interest payments on private capital investments, or by direct investment by the state. Governments may also actively support certain areas of the economy by promoting monopolistic conditions. This was certainly the case in Germany during the last 25 years of the nineteenth century when the state encouraged the formation of huge cartels in major industries such as coal, iron and steel, cement, chemicals and electricity. Within each industry there was no competition, with prices and wages standardised. It is extremely important to note that the economic thinking behind this form of intervention is the very opposite of the free-market perspective. Whereas the latter sees competition as highly desirable, as the key to rapid economic growth, the German model, by actively reducing the scope for competition, seeks consciously to avoid the uncertainty produced by the vagaries of the market.

The fourth way in which the state can promote industrialisation is by actually owning and operating certain core industries. This was mainly confined to railways, which in Belgium and Russia and parts of Germany were owned and run by the state. In France the railways were a joint public/ private undertaking. In Britain, by contrast, the expansion of the rail network from the 1840s on was financed entirely by private capital with no state involvement.

Last, in discussing the diffusion of industrialism it will be useful at this point to say something briefly about the case of Japan.

Until the middle of the nineteenth century Japan had existed in a condition of self-imposed isolation from the rest of the world. In the 1850s the Western powers, led by the United States, forced the Japanese to open their ports to foreign trade. The hostility this humiliation provoked within the country trigerred a national revival which resulted in 1868 in the restoration of the Meiji emperor. (During the previous feudal era the emperor had had virtually no formal authority, being largely a symbolic figure.) The new leaders who supported the restoration quickly grasped that national strength and integrity could only be secured through rapid social and economic development. In 1869 the feudal system was formally abolished and with it the privileges of its samurai warriors. Students were sent in large numbers to Europe and America to study Western technology and culture. Fundamental Japanese institutions – the system of government, the civil service, the judicial system, the army and education – were consciously remodelled along Western lines. A massive programme of state-sponsored industrialisation was embarked upon. By the 1880s textile industries had developed on a significant scale. As with continental Europe, but in marked contrast with Britain, we note the extensive involvement of the Japanese state in that country's industrialisation and modernisation.

Europe was generally fortunate in that the basic ores and minerals needed for the early stages of the Industrial Revolution, coal and iron, were deposited in sufficient quantities in Europe itself. But as industrialisation progressed other materials were needed which either could not be found there in sufficient quantities or were completely absent. With the development of electricity, for example, large quantities of tin and copper were needed. The appearance of the internal combustion engine significantly increased the demand for oil. Electricity and the automobile together vastly augmented the demand for rubber. For all these materials Europe became increasingly dependent upon the non-industrialised world. By the end of the nineteenth century Britain was self-sufficient only in coal, depending upon overseas supplies for most of its timber, wool, an increasing proportion of its iron ore and all of its cotton, petroleum and rubber. In fact by the turn of the century an international division of labour had been firmly established in which the industrialised countries imported primary products from their non-industrialised counterparts and exported to the latter manufactured goods and capital equipment. This type of exchange has determined the character of the world economy for most of this century. Although such a division of labour may appear rational, indeed natural, its rationality seems to have worked to the advantage of the industrialised world, for this division of labour is emphatically Eurocentric: expressly geared to the needs of Europe and its peoples. It was made possible only by the European powers arrogating to themselves, through conquest and colonisation, vast areas of the world's surface.

THE INTERNATIONAL DIVISION OF LABOUR: NORTH AND SOUTH

As indicated at the beginning of this chapter Europe in the fifteenth century was by no means the most advanced area in the world. Many of the vast array of societies in the rest of the world were probably on a par with those of Europe at that time. During the next three hundred years, however, northern Europe was to make such stupendous advances economically, politically and culturally that it left the rest of the world behind. A crucial factor in Europe's advance was its ability through military superiority – itself a reflection of technological ascendance – to gain control of world trade and of areas which produced both the commodities and the media of trade – the spices, the sugar, the cotton, the tobacco, the slaves and the gold and silver. As a result of this process of *incorporation* the economies of Africa, Asia and Latin America became effectively satellites of European and subsequently North American economies. That is to say, the economic systems which preexisted European contact were 'broken open' and harnessed to the needs of the core economies of the industrialised North. Peasants who had previously produced primarily for their own subsistence found themselves constrained by a variety of pressures to produce cash crops such as peanuts or cotton, now needed in the factories of Europe. Other peasant farmers were forced to undertake paid employment in European plantations or mines in order to earn the cash to pay the taxes the Europeans imposed on them.

For many writers the fact that the economies of the South were incorporated on 'dependent' terms into the economic systems of the North is at the heart of the stark inequalities that exist today between the two spheres. Such writers would point out that it is no accident that the one area of the non-European world that was able to resist European penetration, Japan, is the only non-European country to have become a major industrial power.

The dependency argument is controversial and it is not necessary that we attempt to review it in this book. Suffice it to say that the industrialised world still gets most of its raw materials and a good deal of its food from the non-industrialised South. The South provides us with much of our copper, tin, iron ore, bauxite, timber, uranium, oil, rubber and cotton; our rice, coffee, cocoa, fruit, beans and sugar. Conversely the less-developed countries (LDCs) of the South continue to form a major market for our capital and manufactured goods: from machine tools, furnaces, generators, locomotives and finished steel to motor cars, washing-machines, teapots, drinking-glasses, Scotch whisky and electric irons. This dependence upon overseas sources for capital and manufactured goods reflects the fact that most of the countries of Latin America, the Caribbean, Africa, Asia and the Pacific are poorly equipped to produce these goods themselves.

First, we need to understand that when considering 'the South' or 'LDCs' we are dealing with a vast range of societies which differ from each other almost as much as they do from developed countries. In an attempt to convey some of this diversity the World Bank in its annual *World Development Report* distinguishes between 'low-income economies' which in 1985 had an average annual income per head of $270; 'middle-income economies' with an average of $820–1290; and 'upper-middle-income economies' with an average of $1850. This last category includes some southern European countries such as Greece and Yugoslavia. It overlaps with 'industrial market economies' which had an average income per head of $11 810. The United States topped the list of 19 industrialised countries with Britain in fourteenth place.

Despite the diversity it should be apparent from these figures and from the diagram below that the volume of material wealth that is produced in LDCs is considerably less than in industrialised countries. In fact the proportion of the population which is actually living in poverty may be as high as 40 per cent and is seldom less than 20 per cent.

This restricted ability to produce goods and services is explained primarily by the fact that the modern technologies which have permitted massive increases in the production of material goods are not widely dispersed in LDCs. For a start a majority of the labour force work in agriculture: 74 per cent in Bangladesh, 69 per cent in India, 60 per cent in Zimbabwe and 50 per cent in El Salvador. By contrast only three of the World Bank's 19 industrialised countries have more than 10 per cent of their labour forces in agriculture (Ireland, Spain and Italy). Furthermore, the agriculture that predominates in LDCs is not the highly mechanised, capital-intensive farming

Figure 2.1   Per capita gross national product in selected countries

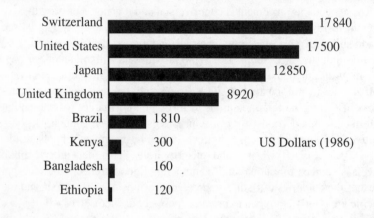

Source: Michael P. Todaro (1989) *Economic Development in the Third World* (London: Longman) p. 29.

of the industrialised world with its enormous prairies, combine harvesters and huge grain silos. Third world agriculture is generally speaking *peasant* agriculture: small plots of land, family labour, production mainly for subsistence and very little in the way of labour-saving technology. Millions of peasants throughout the world must earn their living from the soil without even the benefit of draught animals for pulling ploughs. The hoe, the machete and human muscle power still constitute the bulk of the labour input of a majority of the world's farmers. Furthermore, the peasant farmer does not have access to the scientific inputs and technological advantages enjoyed by the farmer in the industrialised North: the fertilisers, weed-killers, pest-control agents, veterinary services and such like. In addition the typical LDC suffers from poor infrastructure which seriously disadvantages agriculture as well as other areas of the economy. That is to say, LDCs tend to have bad roads and poor transport facilities generally. Electricity, crucial in farming for drying and refrigeration, is largely unavailable outside the towns. Adequate buildings for storing produce and reliable irrigation facilities are in extremely short supply. All this results in low productivity in agriculture which in turn has a number of important consequences. First, agricultural producers and their families do not get enough to eat, which impairs their capacity to work as well as rendering them susceptible to illness and disease. Not only peasant farmers but the population generally in LDCs are undernourished. The World Bank calculates that whereas the daily per capita intake of food in the UK in 1981 was 132 per cent of the basic minimum, in Brazil it was 109 per cent, in India 87 per cent and in Bangladesh 84 per cent. Life expectancy in the UK in 1981 was 74, in Brazil 64, in India 52 and in Bangladesh 48. It should be pointed out that these are averages and that since, for a variety of reasons, inequalities in LDCs are much more marked than in DCs, the calorie intake and life expectancy of the majority will be a good deal lower than these figures indicate.

The second consequence of low levels of agricultural productivity is that insufficient food is produced to meet the needs of a rapidly expanding population. LDCs generally have experienced over the past 25 years heavy migration to their towns and cities. The urban population of LDCs is increasing by around 4–6 per cent per annum whereas the rate for the industrialised 19 is seldom more than 2 per cent and in most cases is 1 per cent or less. These migrants are drawn to the shanty towns and squatter settlements of third world cities by the search for alternatives to the interminable drudgery of peasant agriculture. Increasingly they are being driven out of the agricultural sector as land to which they had had customary access is bought out or appropriated by large landowners or international corporations to be used for the production of tobacco, pineapples, cocoa, cotton or other cash crops.

Now these urban masses, or at least enough of them if serious upheavals are to be avoided, must be able to buy food at prices they can afford. This means that most LDC governments are forced not only to import food but also subsidise basics like bread and rice so that they are within the reach of enough urban dwellers. Importing food means using up valuable foreign exchange acquired through the sale of primary commodities – copper, sisal, coffee, rubber – a crucial part of LDCs' meagre resource endowment. This foreign exchange could have been used to buy capital equipment from the industrialised world in order to establish or refurbish infant industries, thereby reducing the dependence on imported manufactures as well as increasing the productive capacity of the economy. The funds absorbed by food subsidies could have been devoted to improving the infrastructure and hence overall levels of productivity. The need to import and subsidise food has usually provoked balance of payments crises, forcing LDCs to borrow overseas, latterly at high rates of interest. Far from resolving economic problems, the burden of debt-servicing – paying of interest and principal – has invariably exacerbated them. Under such circumstances capital formation, the accumulation and investment of capital in factories, machines and raw materials, is severely inhibited. The amount of capital generated in a low-productivity economy, just like a low-productivity firm, is limited anyway.

Furthermore, in an uncertain market the incentive to invest in manufacturing ventures which will yield a profit only in the long term is low. Such capital as is available tends to flow into property overseas or Swiss bank accounts; or, if locally, into trading and the services sector: importing, renting houses, running taxis and lorries, where the yields tend to be quicker.

We must also remember when we look at the small indigenous manufacturing sector in most LDCs that it has to compete with a much longer-established, considerably more sophisticated and better-organised manufacturing sector emanating from the industrialised world. This means that not only must local manufacturers compete with imports that are cheaper and better than they can produce, but also increasingly with products made locally under the auspices of multinational corporations. The multinational corporation (MNC), the business organisation which transcends national boundaries, is the institutional embodiment of a *world* economy. The MNC has had such a significant impact on *all* the national economies of the world that its introduction merits a separate section of this chapter.

THE MULTINATIONAL CORPORATION

International companies have existed for centuries. Banking has been conducted across international boundaries since the Middle Ages and in the fifteenth and sixteenth centuries large joint-stock companies such as the East India Company organised long-distance trade across the world. In the nineteenth century companies from Britain, Europe and the United States continued to operate large international trading concerns whilst others ran public utilities such as railways, gas and electricity in foreign countries. But from around 1860 manufacturing companies began to establish production facilities outside their own countries. As early as 1865 the German Friedrich Bayer had taken a share in an aniline plant in New York State. The following year the Swedish inventor of dynamite, Alfred Nobel, set up an explosives plant in Hamburg. And in 1867 Singer built its first overseas plant in Glasgow. Since it was the first company to mass-market a standard product bearing the same name across the world, Singer may have a strong claim to being the world's first true multinational.

Several factors lay behind this type of corporate expansion. The communications revolution already mentioned encouraged the development of MNCs in at least two ways: first, improvements in transport greatly accelerated the process of urbanisation and hence the growth of accessible mass markets; and second, the development of telegraph and telephone communication made it possible for headquarters to maintain speedy and regular contacts with subsidiaries. But the most important reason for the development of international firms in the last decades of the nineteenth century was the spread of protectionism. Britain apart, industrialising states everywhere introduced tariffs in order to promote the growth of indigenous industries by protecting them from outside competition. The existence of such tariffs provided a powerful incentive for overseas companies to produce locally and so avoid paying them.

During the early stages of the emergence of the international corporation American companies played a leading role. This was primarily because of the sheer size of American business enterprises. During the 1880s and 1890s US industry went through a remarkable process of concentration under which 5000 companies were eventually consolidated into around 300 trusts. As a result of the intense and often ruthless competition that lay behind this process of consolidation American management acquired invaluable experience in thinking and planning on a large scale. Consequently the shift from operating over the vast distances of the North American continent to the other side of the Atlantic did not demand a radical change in management practices. As Stephen Hyner (in Hugo Radice, *International Firms and Modern Imperialism*, 1979) has succinctly put it, 'In becoming national firms US corporations learned how to become international.' The fact that their sophisticated management techniques made it possible for these increasingly large corporations to earn high profits in the USA placed them in a strong position to start up branches overseas. The overseas offspring could be subsidised by its parent until it cut its teeth in an unfamiliar setting. These subsidiaries often moved into the new territory on a very large scale. In 1901 Westinghouse was the largest industrial concern in Britain, and Standard Oil the largest oil company in Europe. By 1924 Ford was producing one-quarter of the cars made in Britain. However the predominance of American corporations should not lead us to ignore movements in the other direction from Europe to America. By 1914 some European companies had achieved a leading position in certain areas of the US economy – Courtaulds in the rayon industry, Lever Brothers in soap manufacture, for example. Nonetheless, the enormous size of the US economy meant that such activities could be absorbed whereas the operations of US subsidiaries in Europe were much more visible. Even by the turn of the century fears were publicly expressed in Europe about this new form of invasion.

Nonetheless, at this stage in the development of the international economy, the vast proportion of capital movements still took the form of portfolio investments, that is to say, individuals or institutions buying shares in overseas companies for the purpose of making a profit. These shareholders played no role in the actual operation of the enterprise in question. For example, most of the stock in US railway companies before 1914 was owned by Britons but these Britons played no part whatsoever in the actual management of the railways. Modern MNCs, by contrast, make direct investments; they set up subsidiaries which they own and *control* in foreign countries. The activities of these subsidiaries are closely directed from the metropolitan headquarters. In fact, it is argued that the extent to which policy is centralised is the essential characteristic of the MNC. Head office evolves a global corporate strategy, deciding on the location of new investment, the allocation of export markets and research programmes to its affiliates. Affiliates operate according to the policy directives laid down under the MNC's global strategy, the basic aim of which is to increase market share. The activities of MNCs have aroused considerable disquiet because of the enormous resources which the largest among them are able to deploy. In 1980 the four largest MNCs together had an annual turnover greater than the total GNP of the whole continent of Africa. The top 34 corporations have global production in excess of the total production of some 80 LDCs in which over half the world's population lives.

MNCs are overwhelmingly oligopolistic in character, which is to say that they dominate in markets where there are a few large sellers. Competition through price-cutting is not a feature of oligopolistic markets where firms compete rather through product innovation and differentiation, marketing strategies and brand identification. The key to the power and influence of the MNC lies in its control of 'knowledge'. By 'knowledge' we are obviously referring to technological know-how as expressed in 'hard' machinery and equipment. But equally important is the 'soft' technology of marketing, advertising, data control, management training and so forth. The MNC derives its impetus from its ability to convert knowledge into commercially viable projects. In fact there is a view that *the* crucial resource of the MNC is not the actual ownership of assets, but its ability to create, commercialise and retain control of relevant applied knowledge. Proponents of this view have observed that the increasing tendency of LDC governments to own or part-own the capital stock of large international companies – whether as a result of outright nationalisation or joint-venture agreements – has not significantly diminished their dependence.

The question of whether the MNC has increased the dependence of LDCs on the industrialised world is one that we cannot even attempt to resolve in this book. The main point to note in relation to MNCs is the pronounced tendency in the past decade or so for manufacturing under their auspices to be shifted from developed to less-developed economies. It should be understood that historically the extractive sector, especially

petroleum and mining, has been the most important area of foreign investment in LDCs. The control of sources of raw materials – oil, copper,
rubber, tin, vegetable oils – was initially the primary factor behind direct
foreign investment. However, there has recently been a shift from mining
and petroleum in favour of manufacturing and utilities and services (for
example, banking, transport, tourism, advertising). Two basic factors lie
behind this shift. First, because control of vital natural resources such as oil
has been such an explosive political issue, there has been rising pressure on
LDC governments to assert national rights over such resources. As a result
MNCs have been constrained to accept outright nationalisation, joint
ventures, franchising and the like. A major consequence has been the
movement of MNCs into the processing of raw materials locally.

The second factor is the availability in LDCs of supplies of cheap labour.
One of the main reasons for the direct investment of American companies in
Europe, particularly in the postwar boom period, was the abundant supply
of cheap labour. As the price of European labour increased in the 1960s, so
MNCs began to look for alternative locations for manufacturing activities
which required unskilled labour. As a result the stereotype of the LDC as an
exporter of primary products and importer of manufactures had to be questioned as we progressed through the 1970s. Whereas manufactures constituted only 16 per cent of the exports of LDCs in 1965, by 1980 they had
increased to over a quarter to 26 per cent. This 26 per cent is of course an
average figure for all LDCs and therefore obscures the development of a
very striking manufacturing capacity in certain 'newly industrialising countries' (NICs) such as Hong Kong, Singapore, Malaysia, Taiwan, Argentina,
Brazil and Mexico (see Box 2.1 overleaf). Some impression of the extent to
which economies such as that of Brazil have developed over the past twenty
years may be gathered from the fact that in the late 1980s the Royal Air
Force ordered 130 wholly-Brazilian-engineered training aircraft.

The accelerating shift of manufacturing capacity away from what has
traditionally been regarded as the industrial heartland is of major significance. It suggests that what have hitherto been regarded as the *industrial*
economies are in fact ceasing to be industrial. The implications of the
emergence of what has been termed 'post-industrial society' we shall be
looking at in some detail towards the end of this book.

CONCLUSION

We have seen that from the sixteenth century on there developed a world
economy at the centre of which stood northern Europe, particularly Britain,

Box 2.1 Newly industrialising countries (NICs)

From the late sixties a number of countries in the third world and on the European periphery experienced greatly accelerated rates of industrialisation. There is no definitive list of these NICs but the following countries are usually held to constitute the core: Brazil, Mexico, South Korea, Hong Kong, Singapore and Taiwan. (Greece, Spain and Portugal are also sometimes included.) The key factor in identifying a NIC is growth in manufacturing output. Four of these nine had growth rates in the seventies exceeding 9 per cent per year, 3 exceeded 6 per cent and 2 exceeded 3 per cent. (The figure for Taiwan is unknown.) The NICs have concentrated on export-oriented industrialisation and have sought investment by making local conditions particularly attractive for international capital. These conditions usually include duty-free entry for goods for assembly, fewer restrictions on profit transfer, lower company taxation, reduced pollution restraints together with restrictions on labour organisation (banning strikes, and so on), thereby creating a cheap labour force. In 1965 no LDC figured among the world's top 30 exporters of manufactured goods. By 1985 Hong Kong and South Korea were among the top 15 with export shares close to those of Sweden and Switzerland. Singapore and Brazil were among the top 20 with export shares close to those of Denmark and Finland.

France and Holland. As trade and commerce expanded, this Eurocentred economy drew more and more areas of the world into its orbit. The pattern of trade that came to be established was one in which Europe supplied the rest of the world with manufactures whilst the rest of the world furnished Europe with raw materials. This emerging pattern was firmly consolidated after the Industrial Revolution which so increased the productive capacity of the system as to undermine remaining areas of manufacturing outside Europe. India and China, whose handicraft industries had long supplied European markets, are notable examples. Thus was established a basic international division of labour whose consequences are still evident in the striking contrasts between the developed and the less-developed worlds today.

The global nature of the international economy expresses itself at the levels of both production and consumption. As we saw at the beginning of this chapter the commodities which the system produces combine inputs from all over the world. But in terms of consumption also, an increasing proportion of goods and services – whether we are talking about automobiles, personal stereos, soft drinks, jeans, films or soap operas – are produced for a *world* market. Thus a major consequence of the emergence of a world economy has been the globalisation of products and styles.

Undoubtedly the ability to consume these goods and services varies enormously between countries. We in the (as yet) prosperous West are immensely more fortunate in this respect than most of our counterparts in Africa, Asia, Latin America and the former Soviet bloc. But irrespective of the ability to consume, the culture of consumerism is diffused throughout the globe. Even in the remotest parts of the world – the Amazonian rainforests, the desert margins of West Africa, the tiny islands of the Indonesian archipelago – there can be few individuals who are totally unaware of the material culture which holds such away over our lives. As suggested in this chapter, one of the distinctive features of this material culture is that it is produced by a capitalist system and it is to the question of the essential character of capitalism that we turn in the next chapter.

BIBLIOGRAPHY

Frank, A. G.(1978) *World Accumulation 1492–1789* (London: Macmillan).
Hobsbawm, E. J.(1986) *Industry and Empire* (Harmondsworth: Penguin).
Hopkins, A. G.(1980) *An Economic History of West Africa* (London: Longman).
Radice, H.(1979) *International Firms and Modern Imperialism* (Harmondsworth: Penguin).
Rostow, W. W.(1962) *The Stages of Economic Growth: A Non-Communist Manifesto* (Cambridge: Cambridge University Press).
The Times Atlas of World History (1984) (London: Times Books).
Todaro, M. P.(1989) *Economic Development of the Third World* (London: Longman).
Tugendhat, C.(1973) *The Multinationals* (Harmondsworth: Penguin).
World Development Report 1986 (Oxford University Press).

3 Capitalism and Industrialism

It was suggested in the previous chapter that an industrial economy is one in which inanimate sources of power are harnessed to the production of material goods. Technological advances in the eighteenth century, the introduction of new types of machinery and the development of steam power, vastly increased the productive capacity of the economy. But merely producing more is of little benefit unless what is produced can be consumed. Accordingly industrialisation was fundamentally associated with the development of *markets* for the sale of the goods which the system could now produce. Without these markets, without the possibility of selling the goods, the pioneering industrialists – factory owners, ironfounders, railway builders – would hardly have invested money, time and energy in bringing together factors of production and organising the productive system. In other words, the prospect of making a *profit* was and is the salient feature of the capitalist system; in fact the driving force behind it. This is a very important point since there have been industrial societies where the profit motive is not the central principle of organisation. In the Soviet bloc countries, prior to its breakup, the *needs of their citizens* and not profit theoretically provided the rationale behind what was produced and how it was distributed. *Socialist* industrial societies have centrally planned economies in which factors of production and goods and services are allocated on the basis of planning decisions rather than the market forces of supply and demand. Accordingly, *capitalist* industrial societies are those whose economies are organised to mass-produce goods and services for profit. However this statement is in need of a good deal of further qualification and it is precisely the aim of this chapter to bring out the essential features of capitalist industrial societies. The point being made in this introductory section is that the terms 'capitalist' and 'industrial' are not necessarily synonymous. Industrial societies need not be capitalist and capitalist societies are not necessarily industrial. In order to bring out the shades of meaning behind these deceptively simple terms it will be useful to look, first of all, at a type of society which was neither capitalist nor industrial.

FEUDALISM

The term 'feudalism' refers to a phase of development through which many areas of Europe passed from the ninth century until, in some cases, the nineteenth. Feudalism emerged out of the 'Dark Ages', the turbulent four hundred years during which the Roman Empire disintegrated and Europe was battered by successive waves of invasion from the east and the north. This was a period in which the state, in the sense of a central government maintaining law and order and administering justice, virtually ceased to exist. It was an age during which trade and commerce declined drastically because of prevailing insecurity; when social and economic life, for reasons of safety, tended to shift away from the towns to rural communities. Feudalism, the system which began to crystallise from around 800 on, was a response to the profound crisis that had afflicted European society over the previous four centuries. This crisis required that the local community, as far as possible, be self-sufficient, in terms of providing not only its material needs, but also its own government.

The basic socioeconomic unit of feudal society was therefore the *fief*, the landed estate or manor that was granted to a member of the warrior aristocracy by the monarch or some powerful lord in return for military service. This warrior class, being of noble status, did not 'work', that is, perform manual labour, but fought as required and provided protection for those too weak, in those dangerous times, to look after themselves. Since they did not produce their own material needs these had to be provided by the class the aristocracy allegedly protected, the peasantry – in fact the overwhelming majority of the population.

Generally speaking, a fief, or estate or manor, would incorporate a village community, associated with which was an area of arable land as well as common or waste land which was used for rough grazing, the collection of firewood and hunting small animals and birds. Part of the arable land was reserved for the lord of the manor and was called the 'demesne'. The remainder was allocated in the form of strips to members of the village community. However, in return for the strip of land on which he grew his food, each villager had to render 'services' to his lord. Each week a certain number of days' labour must be performed on the lord's demesne. In addition to these labour services certain obligatory payments or taxes had to be made. These and other obligations signified the peasant's or *serf's* servile or unfree status. So far as the aristocracy was concerned the peasant had no rights, not even rights of property: in theory his land and livestock belonged to his lord and could be alienated from him. But perhaps the most forceful expression of the serf's lack of freedom was his inability to leave the estate. He and his family were tied or 'bonded' to it by law for life as had been their ancestors and as would be their descendants. This, then, was a society in which each person's position or status was fixed and narrowly cicumscribed in law and custom even to the extent of what clothes they could wear, the weapons they could carry and the foods they could consume.

At the risk of some simplification we may identify the following three principal characteristics of feudalism. First, it was an overwhelmingly agrarian society in that a large majority of the population was supported, either directly or indirectly, by agriculture. However, this was not the agriculture that we are used to in modern industrial societies – heavily mechanised and capital-intensive with production for the market. Agriculture under feudalism was peasant agriculture: a form of agriculture in which family labour using simple tools and techniques produces primarily for its own subsistence. That is to say, the peasant family worked its strips of land to produce the food it needed to survive. But in addition the peasant family had to produce a surplus over and above its consumption needs to meet its tax obligations to the lord. It also had to provide labour for the lord's demesne. This brings us to the second essential characteristic of feudal society: the fact that it is presided over by a ruling class which takes no part in but is supported by this agricultural system. This is because this ruling class is able to use its political power (ultimately force) to appropriate part of the surplus produced by a captive peasantry. The surplus could be in kind or cash, or take the form of labour services. Feudalism's third essential characteristic was that the basic exchanges which underpinned the system were *personal* rather than monetary. The serf did not pay rent in money for the land which he and his family worked, but performed labour services for his lord. Conversely the lord did not pay wages for the work done on his demesne but gave out strips of land (as well as performing certain civic functions and maintaining law and order). Again the peasant farmer did not pay wages to those who worked his land with him since these were members of his family. Ties of kinship rather than cash payment secured him a labour force. Whereas we are paid wages for the work we perform and pay in cash for the bulk of the goods and services we require, the majority of the population of feudal England derived most of what they needed through a network of personal ties. This is not to argue that monetary exchange was entirely absent from feudal society: we have already seen that the serf had to render some of his dues in cash. He would also need cash to purchase some of the items or services which his peasant farm could not produce: salt, charcoal or the services of smiths, wheelwrights or thatchers, for example. In order to raise this cash, a portion of the food he grew would have to be sold in local markets. Despite these transactions the feudal economy was undoubtedly dominated by personal exchanges, that is, by exchanges between persons who are bound in some form of social relationship, for example, father–son, lord–peasant.

TOWNS AND TRADE

Although the feudal system was overwhelmingly agrarian, being composed of a large number of inward-looking, self-governing rural communities, trade and urban life never entirely died out even in the Dark Ages. As we have seen, the peasant had to sell some of his produce to obtain the cash he needed to meet his tax obligations as well as to pay for necessities. Much of this produce – raw materials such as wool and hides as well as food – found its way to the town. As the feudal system consolidated itself and the security situation improved, so the volume of trade expanded and with it the scope of urban life. Urbanisation – the tendency of economic and social activity to move from countryside to town – expressed itself in a more complex division of labour, especially in extending the range of occupations outside agriculture. In addition to the merchants who organised the movement and sale of commodities were the trades associated with transportation – carters, wheelwrights, farriers, harness-makers. Craftsmen were needed to transform raw materials into commodities – bakers, brewers, tailors, saddlers. Urban life called for larger and more sophisticated buildings, hence an expansion in the crafts associated with construction: bricklayers, stonemasons, glaziers. And an increase in the volume of business transactions generated a need for more lawyers, copiers, moneylenders, bankers, brokers and contractors of various kinds. These occupations, it is emphasised, did not suddenly appear in the eleventh century. Virtually all of them had existed in ancient Greece and Rome and many of them had emerged thousands of years before in the wake of the neolithic revolution. What was happening in Europe in the eleventh and twelfth centuries was the beginnings of a long-drawn-out shift from a relatively simple rural economy geared mainly for subsistence towards a much more complex urban economy oriented to the market.

CAPITALISM

It has been argued that 'capitalism' entails the production of goods or the provision of services for profit. This, however, will not serve to identify capitalism as a distinctive system since throughout human history individuals and groups have exchanged goods and services with others with a view to striking a good bargain. Even though many of these transactions were barter exchanges and did not involve money as conventionally understood, this does not mean that economic calculation was entirely absent; that this was some form of irrational exchange. It would be somewhat arrogant of us to assume that the Congo pygmy who exchanges gourds for steel axes with his Bantu neighbour is oblivious of the customary ratio of gourds to axes. If we look at the more complex civilisations of the ancient world from Sumeria to Greece and Rome, it is quite apparent that the use of money was widespread, trade extensive, and that traders and merchants amassed huge fortunes in money or goods – 'capital' as it came to be known in the late Middle Ages. Does this mean that capitalism has existed since the dawn of civilisation? In a sense the answer to this question is in the affirmative in that the seeds of capitalism are to be found in the propensity in human nature 'to truck, barter and exchange one thing for another', as Adam Smith put it in *The Wealth of Nations*. Nonetheless, to help us grasp more clearly the course of social and economic development, it is necessary to limit the application of the term to a discernible pattern of social and economic relationships. First, most social scientists would agree that a central feature of a capitalist society is that 'capital' is privately owned. By capital we mean not just money but more especially 'means of production', that is, the means to produce material goods and services, for example, land, iron hoes, electronic assembly lines. This notion of private ownership of the means of production as a central feature of capitalism should not arouse controversy. Less familiar, perhaps, will be what many see as a second essential characteristic – the existence of a 'free' labour force. That is to say a labour force which is free to sell its labour power wherever it wishes. Hence the *Encyclopaedia Britannica*:

> Fundamental to any system called capitalist are the relations between private owners of non-personal means of production (land, mines, industrial plants, etc., collectively known as capital) and free but capital-less workers who sell their labour services to employers.

Let us look closely at this definition. First, if we consider the idea of owners of non-personal means of production it may be apparent that the feudal lords we discussed above were the owners of the means of production in feudal society – land. Furthermore, this landed nobility was able to maintain itself in fine style because it was able to appropriate a surplus from the estate which it controlled. That is to say, part of what the tied peasantry produced, whether in the form of foodstuffs, taxes or labour, was appropriated by the feudal lord. What is the difference, we need to ask, between a surplus appropriated in this way and the profit taken by the modern businessman? Although there are some similarities, sociologists would maintain that there is nonetheless a pronounced difference in the way in which surplus is appropriated from the labour of the serf on the one hand and from the wage labourer on the other.

Under feudalism surplus is extracted from a captive labour force by means of political compulsion; what some writers would term 'extra-economic coercion'. That is, the feudal nobility ultimately had the power and authority to force the peasantry to yield up its surplus. The wage labourer, by contrast, although under the compulsion of economic necessity, is formally *free* to sell his labour where he chooses. The owner of the means of production, the capitalist, retains his labour not through political compulsion, but by means of the wages he is prepared to pay.

The distinction between pre-capitalist and capitalist forms of labour will become clearer if we look at another element in the above definition which, we note, refers not just to 'free' but also to 'capital-less' labour. Now, a further distinguishing feature about the mediaeval peasant is that he had direct access to the means of production, the strips of land granted to him by his lord, plus the use of village commons, waste land, woods and so on; all of which he could utilise to provide the wherewithal to support his family. The wage earner, by contrast, has no such access as the means of production are in the hands of the capitalist class. Being 'capital-less', the wage worker or 'proletarian' has no alternative but to sell his labour, his only resource, for a wage. Under capitalism labour power becomes a commodity, the price of which is determined by market forces. It follows from this that a crucial stage in the development of capitalism was the separation of the peasantry from its principal means of production – land – as this permitted the formation of a property-less proletariat. This process of 'proletarianisation' we shall return to shortly. Let us conclude this section by provisionally defining capitalism as 'a socio-economic system in which the means of production, distribution and exchange are privately owned by a capitalist class which employs free wage labour to produce goods or services for the market for profit'.

Two further points need to be made. First, the process of transition from feudalism to capitalism was extraordinarily complex and cannot detain us here. Suffice it to say that the essence of this process was the gradual replacement of feudal relations based upon personal exchanges by capitalist relations based upon the market, the 'cash nexus'. In other words, a process in which a small monetised enclave gradually expands to incorporate the subsistence sector rather as a huge crater slowly fills up with water until its cracked and inert surface dissolves and is completely submerged under a (capitalist) lake.

The second important point about the decline of feudalism and the rise of capitalism is that the process varied very significantly from one European society to another. Whereas English feudalism was virtually dead by the time Henry VIII ascended the throne in 1509, in France it survived until the Revolution in 1789, whilst in Germany and Russia (and Japan) the institution was not formally abolished until well into the nineteenth century. The nature and timing of the transition, it is usually agreed, was to have profound consequences for the essential character of these respective modern industrial states.

INDUSTRIALISM

Does it make sense to talk about 'industry' in societies we label 'pre-industrial'? What do we mean by industry? Well, we usually mean the use of mechanical devices to manufacture goods. The problem is that it is far from easy to decide at what point we could call a contrivance a mechanical device. A hunter's knife? Probably not. A carpenter's saw worked by a foot pedal? Possibly. A grindstone driven by a water-wheel would be less of a problem as here we are able to identify what we usually understand by 'machinery'. However, a seemingly endless process of classifying devices as mechanical or not does not really help our discussion along a great deal. It is better to accept that some form of industry exists in all societies in the sense of transforming raw materials into artefacts, and proceed to try and identify certain basic types of industry. In fact, four basic types seem to suggest themselves: *household industry*; *handicraft industry*; *domestic* or *'putting out' industry*; and *centralised production*.

Household industry

The peasant family must clearly engage in activities outside the immediate tasks of agricultural production. The farm's stock of capital must be maintained and renewed: implements, fences, dwellings, outbuildings and so on. In addition, agricultural commodities must be processed for family consumption: corn milled and baked, or brewed or distilled; textiles made from wool or flax; animal skins fashioned into leather items; wood into tools; timber into building materials, or charcoal for burning. Household industry has two basic characteristics. First, it is integrated into the agricultural economy, is in fact an adjunct of this economy. This means that the amount of time that can be allotted to household industry is largely contingent upon the agricultural season. More of it will be done during slack periods in the agricultural cycle. The second basic characteristic is that the producers consume what they themselves produce. In sociological parlance the spheres of production and consumption are *not differentiated*. To the extent that such differentiation develops, that is, where some items are sold to neighbours or in nearby markets, we are moving towards the second type.

Handicraft industry

This involves the craftsman working full-time using simple tools to transform raw materials into commodities for sale. In addition to members of his family the craftsman or artisan may be assisted by living-in apprentices as well as employing the services of day labourers. Handicraft production has the following four basic characteristics: the means of production are small-scale and inexpensive which means that very little capital is required and separate 'factory' buildings are not needed to house them; second, power is supplied by human or animal muscle supplemented, where possible, by wind and water; third, artisan occupations are differentiated from agricultural pursuits although integrated into the agricultural economy in that the latter supplies raw materials – meat, corn, wool, timber, leather; last, the spheres of production and consumption are not separated: consumers will tend to live locally and be known personally to the craftsman. In other words, the producer here is in close social contact with his market.

Domestic industry

Domestic industry, or the 'putting-out' system, shares the basic characteristics of handicraft production except that here we have the appearance of a middleman who supplies raw materials and buys finished goods. The most important difference between domestic industry and the previous category is that the spheres of production and consumption are now more clearly separated. The market is more distant, more anonymous, is now mediated to the craftsman through the person (or persons) of the middleman. This means that the craftsman loses some of his independence as he is locked into a market system whose workings he cannot comprehend and anticipate to the same degree as the artisan producing directly for local markets. He is therefore more vulnerable to the vagaries of market forces. Nonetheless the craftsman at this stage is still an independent producer; he does not work for a wage but produces commodities with his *own* means of production.

Centralised production

This is of course the factory system with which we are most familiar and where the means of production are concentrated around a central source of

power. It is important to understand that forms of centralised production
existed before the Industrial Revolution in areas where the availability of
raw materials or the logic of production dictated. Mining, salt-making and
iron-smelting are examples of the first; shipbuilding and housebuilding (the
great houses of the rich) of the second. By the beginning of the eighteenth
century technological developments in England had promoted the centralisation of production in a number of industries: brewing, brickmaking,
sugar-refining and the manufacture of soap and armaments, for example.
Many establishments in these industries were owned and controlled by
wealthy capitalists employing many hundreds of workers.

The essential point, however, is that whilst it existed before, centralised
production did not become the norm until after the Industrial Revolution, in
fact until well into the second half of the nineteenth century. What vastly
accelerated this already well-established trend were technical innovations,
particularly in textile manufacturing – Kay's 'flying shuttle', Hargreaves's
'spinning jenny', Arkwright's 'water frame' and Crompton's 'mule' –
coupled with the application of steam power to production. The years
1775–1800 saw the rapid dissemination of the Boulton and Watt steam
engine in mining, foundries, forges and breweries, but above all, in cotton
mills. Steam power not only vastly increased the demand for coal but also
for iron machines as wooden ones could not withstand the pace of production. The level of investment needed for such means of production was
clearly beyond the means of. the ordinary craftsman. Furthermore their
scale and complexity demanded that they be housed outside the domestic
situation and that their operation be directly supervised by their owners, the
industrial bourgeoisie.

Before moving on it needs to be emphasised that the rise to predominance of centralised production does not in any sense mean that the other
forms disappeared. On the contrary, not only did most aspects of them
survive into the industrial era, but there is much current speculation that as
we move towards the turn of the century, at least one of them – domestic
industry – is enjoying a revival. This argument we will return to in a later
chapter. In the meantime let us turn to look at the two basic classes that
were created by the Industrial Revolution.

BOURGEOISIE

Technological advance alone could not have made the Industrial Revolution. Some groups of individuals needed to be convinced that the various
inventions could be put to profitable use; that the increases in production

which these developments made possible could actually be sold. In other words a class had to emerge which was prepared not only to invest in the means of production but also to assume responsibility for organising the actual process of production, including the recruitment and coordination of the labour force. Such a class is known as an industrial bourgeoisie. Now the term 'bourgeois' has acquired negative overtones in contemporary usage, usually implying prosperous, self-satisfied, middle-class respectability. So far as social and economic development is concerned, however, 'bourgeoisie' has a specific and neutral meaning. Furthermore, an appreciation of the role of the bourgeoisie and of bourgeois values is essential for a proper understanding not only of the emergence of industrial society, but of its continuing evolution.

Originally the term signified quite simply someone who was a recognised citizen of a town. Hence the merchants and artisans (craftsmen) as well as a miniscule group of educated persons such as lawyers and physicians who lived and worked in the towns during the feudal period constituted the principal elements of a numerically small but nonetheless vigorous bourgeoisie. As feudalism declined the economic and social significance of the bourgeoisie increased. In fact the wealth and influence of its top layers exceeded that of many members of the aristocracy. Wealthier merchants shifted their interests from trade to lending money, initially to the nobility, subsequently to governments. At the other end of the scale was the largest sector of the pre-industrial bourgeoisie, the 'petty bourgeoisie'. This stratum comprised the numerous independent craftsmen and shopkeepers who operated their own enterprises, perhaps with a day labourer or two and living-in apprentices.

It is impossible to decide where the ranks of the petty bourgeoisie and those of what we can term the merchant bourgeoisie began. Obviously one merged into the other. However a rough and ready guideline is that, apart from wealth and status, manual labour figures prominently in the daily routine of the petty bourgeois whereas the merchant was more concerned with calculation, organisation and decision-making. This distinction and the growing complexity of the division of labour as we approach the industrial period can be illustrated if we look briefly at the organisation of production and marketing in the wool industry; in effect Britain's chief industry until the middle of the eighteenth century. Even then, on the eve of the Industrial Revolution, weaving in some parts of the country, notably the West Riding of Yorkshire and East Anglia, was conducted along lines that had changed little in three hundred years: the master weaver bought or grew his own fleeces, had them carded and spun by members of his family and neighbours, employed journeymen in his home to help with the

weaving and then sold the cloth in local markets. But in the south-west of
England a more complex division of labour had existed since Tudor times.
There, in the face of greater demand for woolen cloth, a middleman had
appeared who had amassed enough capital to buy raw wool in large
quantities, distribute it to a network of domestic weavers, collect the
finished articles and market them. In fact by the eighteenth century three
types of middlemen operated in this area of the wool industry. First, there
was the wool dealer who acted as the intermediary between the grazier and
the cottage weaver supplying the latter with raw wool. Second came the
'clothier' who bought the woven cloth and traded it on to a third group of
'drapers' who marketed the product to the final consumer, either in Britain
or overseas. So even as far back as the sixteenth century a capitalist form of
production had emerged in certain areas of Britain, that is to say, a branch
of production where capital played a crucial role either in the purchase of
raw materials or finished goods. The principal difference between the
craftsman and the merchant is that the former had neither the financial
resources to buy raw materials in large quantities, nor the organisational
means to market his goods beyond the local community.

The fundamental point to note here is that the capitalist at this stage is
essentially an *intermediary* or broker between various stages in the process
of production. He did not get involved or invest his capital in the process of
production itself. The means of production are still primarily in the hands
of the small-scale producer: the spinner, the weaver, the dyer, the fuller and
so on. This form of capital, which is *not* sunk in machines or factories but
is used to buy raw materials and finished goods as well as to pay agents and
arrange for transport, is known as *merchant* capital. Merchant capital and
the merchant capitalist were by no means restricted to the wool trade, but
constitute a general type of entrepreneur during the long period of transition in Britain from the break-up of feudalism to the Industrial Revolution.
In this non-involvement in the actual sphere of production lies the fundamental difference between the merchant capitalist and the industrial capitalist who was to spearhead the Industrial Revolution.

But why, we may ask, in the run-up to the Industrial Revolution, did this
merchant bourgeoisie become interested in the actual process of production? Why were its members increasingly willing to sink their capital in
machines, buildings and so fourth? This is an enormously complex
question, one which we can barely touch on here. Part of the answer lies in
technological developments – the inventions that were mentioned earlier.
In addition to these, improved communications and a marked increase in
population made larger markets more accessible. However, in attempting
to answer this question, historians have given increasing emphasis to the

possibilities of control offered by the new factory system. It may be imagined that the putting-out system, where one's producers are scattered in their separate workshops, posed numerous problems of coordination or 'management' for the entrepreneur. How much more convenient if these producers could be brought together under one roof and subjected to direct supervision by the capitalist or his deputy. And even more convenient would it be if these producers were paid a wage for operating someone else's machines. This surely would reduce their independence especially if, in addition, the speed of these machines was determined by a central source of power rather than by the operator's discretion. In other words, a system in which the labour force is made up of capital-less wage earners, increasing the scope for centralised control, offered to simplify immensely the problem of management.

BOURGEOIS REVOLUTION

With the spread of political stability and the growth of the centralised state the military functions of the old feudal aristocracy declined. The aristocratic ethos came to centre on the Court, on courtly behaviour and the cultivation of a distinct set of manners, customs, modes of speech and dress which set them apart from the rest of society. The aristocracy did not work but lived off rents and taxes, in short off the wealth created by others: merchants, craftsmen, farmers, peasants and labourers. Gradually these creators of wealth came to resent more and more the arbitrary exactions of the aristocracy and what increasingly seemed to be their essentially parasitic role in society. Initially, hostility did not take the form of a coherent class critique, but manifested itself in more subtle forms: the support, for example, of the more commercially developed areas of England for the Parliamentary cause against the corruption and absolutism of the King's party during the Civil War period of the seventeenth century. However, with the emergence of a strong industrial bourgeoisie in the first decades of the nineteenth century the conflict assumed much more overtly the aspect of a struggle of one class against another. In a speech in 1845 the Rochdale carpet manufacturer, Quaker and leader of the anti-Corn Law League, John Bright, affirmed his belief that the discontent he helped to articulate was 'a movement of the commercial and industrious classes against the lords and great proprietors of the soil'. A decade before, the rising middle classes had joined forces with their workers to agitate, often violently, against political domination by 'a proud and selfish aristocracy'. In its struggle, during this period, for the reform of parliament the bourgeoisie employed as a weapon its by now substantial economic power, advocating the withdrawal of savings from banks, including the Bank of England. In this proposed action is caught the essence of the struggle between bourgeoisie and aristocracy: the fact that the former, although having built up over the centuries substantial economic power, were still excluded from political power by the aristocracy's monopolistic control of the machine of government. The commonly accepted view is that in the long term economic power will triumph in the sense that those who have most of it will be able to use it to gain control over the state. This may take the form of a literal revolution in the sense of the violent overthrow of the old regime as happened in France in 1789. But in Britain, well into the second half of the nineteenth century, the landed classes were able to retain their grip on the state, that is, central and local government, the civil service and the army. However, a series of legislative acts during the nineteenth century led to the reform of these institutions, the acceptance of the supremacy of market forces and the creation generally of a political environment conducive to bourgeois interests. Consequently when we talk of a bourgeois revolution in Britain we do not mean that the bourgeoisie physically ejected the landed classes from the seat of power, but that the state, by the end of the nineteenth century, had come to represent the interest of trade and industry. Whether those who actually occupied political office or conversely owned factories were of aristocratic or bourgeois background – in fact the two classes had begun to merge long before the Industrial Revolution – is a side issue. Likewise in all European countries, the USA and Japan, although by diverse routes, the state eventually came to represent the interest of private capital.

THE WORK ETHIC

Now, it is obviously the case that throughout history human beings have pursued wealth and riches. Aristocracies and dominant groups in a vast range of societies have invariably striven to appropriate material wealth with a marked degree of enthusiasm. However the idea of a specifically *bourgeois* ethic, for its proponents, means something quite different. Prior to the modern era the accumulation of wealth characteristically manifested itself in lavish projects – ostentatious buildings and monuments, from the pyramids to the Palace of Versailles – all of which expressed the majesty and power of those who had them constructed. Bourgeois accumulation, by contrast, invests wealth not in mausoleums and palaces but ploughs it back into the means of production. Capitalistic activity, according to this view, is informed not by the spirit of ostentation and largesse, but by frugality and restraint.

This type of argument is most evident in an influential and controversial essay by sociologist Max Weber. In *The Protestant Ethic and the Spirit of Capitalism* 1904 Weber attempted to establish a connection between Protestantism and the ideology or 'spirit which he believed was a necessary ingredient for sustained capitalist development. Weber was particularly interested in the Calvinist stream of Protestantism which, while originating in Geneva in the 1530s, manifested itself in Britain in various branches of what became known as 'non-conformity': Puritanism, Baptism, Congregationalism, Presbyterianism and Methodism. Weber shows how basic Calvinist ideas through a complex process of reinterpretation by Puritan preachers were eventually presented in the form of exhortations to Protestants to lead a life of diligence, self-discipline, frugality and hard work. The cultivation of these and other ascetic values became a sign of God's favour, whereas idleness, luxury, extravagance and time-wasting were imputed to the machinations of Satan. The Protestant businessman made money but restrictions on its use meant that there was little option but to reinvest it in the business; hence further accumulation of capital. Economic success was also religious success: so long as his wealth was put to appropriate use the businessman could feel sanctified:

> A specifically bourgeois ethic had grown up. With the consciousness of standing in the fullness of God's grace and being visibly blessed by Him, the bourgeois businessman, as long as he remained within the bounds of formal correctness, as long as his moral conduct was spotless and the use to which he put his wealth was not objectionable, could follow his pecuniary interest as he would and feel that he was fulfilling a duty in doing so. (*The Protestant Ethic and the Spirit of Capitalism*, London, Allen & Unwin, 1976 edn, p. 176–7)

Weber supports his argument with the claim, backed by statistical evidence, that Protestants in Europe were disproportionately represented in the ownership of capital, the upper levels of management and the higher grades of skilled labour. Nonetheless the Weber thesis has been subjected to protracted debate and a good deal of critical comment. This is not the place, however, to become involved in a lengthy examination of the pros and cons of the debate except to mention that even Weber's most trenchant critics are prepared to concede that his argument had a core of truth. More important for our purposes is the observation that the beliefs and values which helped to promote industrial capitalism and were, in turn, promoted by it were those that related success in the world to *individual* effort. The achievement or *work ethic*, commonplace in our own society, made its appearance only very recently in the perspective of human history. It was totally absent from feudal society for example. The feudal nobility did not *earn* their political and economic ascendancy; they enjoyed it as a right, as guardians and protectors of the social order. The peasantry, of course, worked – in fact they worked like donkeys – but any notion that hard work would bring success in life was so alien to their world as to be utterly incomprehensible. Feudalism was, after all, a society in which one's position was inherited and would be passed on to one's heirs. The peasant's lot, therefore, as constantly taught by the clergy, was to endure a life of servitude and hope for salvation after death.

The bourgeoisie, on the other hand, was a class which owed its wealth and position to what it did in the world of trade and commerce. Work for the bourgeoisie could and did bring social advancement even into the ranks of the aristocracy. Accordingly it is not surprising that ideas such as 'achievement', 'self-help' and 'individualism' spring essentially from the bourgeois way of life. Whatever they may think about the Weber thesis, most writers would agree that Protestantism played an important role in the evolution of such ideas. Subsequently wherever capitalism has taken root, such values, although later divested of their religious overtones, have come to dominate social and economic life.

THE EMERGENCE OF AN INDUSTRIAL PROLETARIAT

The term 'proletariat' was originally used to refer to the poor labouring classes of ancient Rome. However, primarily under the influence of Karl Marx, it is not poverty which has become the core feature of the proletariat but being without means of production and consequently having to sell one's labour for a wage. A proletarian thus differs from a peasant as the latter does not work for a wage but cultivates a small plot of land in order to meet his and his family's subsistence needs (as well as his tax obligations). Now a key process in the development of industrial capitalism is 'proletarianisation', the process through which a peasantry, the majority in pre-capitalist society, is transformed into a proletariat, the majority in capitalist society. The character of this transformation varied considerably from one society to another: in Britain it was a prolonged and complex affair in which the peasantry was either gradually pushed out of agriculture by commercial pressures, or, as we get closer to the industrial period, drawn by what seemed to be the high wages paid in the towns. In Germany, by contrast, the abolition of serfdom in 1848 virtually transformed peasant-serfs overnight into agricultural proletarians. The agricultural depression during the last quarter of the nineteenth century forced large numbers of these rural labourers into the towns to form the nucleus of Germany's industrial proletariat. In France yet another pattern displayed itself in which, for a variety of complex reasons, a peasant class was preserved well into the twentieth century. But whatever the path taken to modernity, at the end of it lies a society in which the majority of the population live in towns and cities and sell their labour for a wage.

From the above it will be evident that the elements of a proletariat existed in the urban enclaves of feudal societies where a small number of journeymen as well as general labourers sold their labour for a wage. However, whilst sharing this characteristic with his pre-industrial counterpart, the industrial proletarian had, in addition, to adapt to the work routines of factory life, routines which differed quite radically from those which obtained in a pre-industrial setting. Although the mediaeval peasant endured a life of back-breaking physical toil, the pace at which he and his family worked varied considerably with the time of year. At peak seasons, especially at haymaking and harvest time, work would occupy all daylight hours. During the winter months, on the other hand, there would be little farm labour to do at all. This would be a time for repairing equipment, fences, harnesses and the like, for household industry, as well as for the socialising which was such a dominant feature of village life. The point is that outside those periods when the weather dictated the pace of work, the peasant farmer enjoyed a good deal of discretion over what was to be done and the speed at which it should be done.

In handicraft industry the craftsman was to a considerable degree his own master. Clearly he had to earn enough to keep himself and his family at the level to which they were accustomed. But how the necessary volume of work was actually organised was very much up to him. In other words, if the craftsman chose to work flat out in the mornings and take it easy in the afternoons, or work extra hard on three days leaving the others for relaxation, then he was free to do so. In the putting-out system too, despite greater pressure from market forces, the evidence suggests that work routines were characterised by alternate spurts of industriousness and idleness. In a number of trades Monday was always regarded as a holiday ('St Monday') with little being done on Tuesdays and Wednesdays either. On Thursdays and Fridays the work speeded up to a furious pace in order to fulfil the week's quota.

The crucial point is that the factory system – centralised production – demanded that the labour force be regimented to a degree which had hitherto been confined only to very few areas of production. When all work processes are driven from a single central source of power then they necessarily must be closely interlinked. This means that a shortfall or a surplus of production in one area has knock-on effects throughout that particular enterprise. It is vital, therefore, that work tasks in all departments and sections be carefully synchronised: that workers turn up at the same time, work at a regular pace, do not arbitrarily leave their place of work, have their breaks and leave at the same time and so on. We are so accustomed to the industrial system that these observations may seem trite and unnecessary, but two hundred years ago it is quite clear that the new industrial bourgeoisie confronted a labour force which adapted not at all eagerly to the unrelenting rhythms of factory work. Accordingly the last decades of the eighteenth and first years of the nineteenth centuries are littered with complaints by industrialists about the slovenliness and profligacy of their employees. The essential task confronting them, as one of them, Richard Arkwright, once put it, was to train human beings 'to renounce their desultory habits of work and identify themselves with the unvarying regularity of the complex automaton'.

We shall return later to the details of how labour discipline was eventually drilled into the industrial proletariat. The fundamental point being made in this section is that proletarian labour under the industrial system was not only waged labour, but in addition *timed* labour. For the first time in human history the overwhelming majority of the labour force were subjected to a work routine which was relentless and unceasing, which required a steady input of labour ten or eight hours a day, five or more days a week, and for 48 to 50 weeks a year. The dramatic nature of this transformation is acutely brought out by the historian Christopher Hill when he observes that whereas the worker in 1530 could earn his yearly bread by 14 or 15 weeks' labour, his counterpart two centuries later would need to work 52 weeks to earn the same amount.

Industrialisation then required not simply a revolution in economy and society but also in culture, in the way we perceive and think about the world. It required that long-established practices such as the celebration of saints' days, festivals, fairs and wakes, the socialising, feasting, drinking and carousing that had played such a prominent part in the everyday lives of the 'common people' since time immemorial – that these be eradicated.

This cultural revolution did, of course, take place: by the time of the Great Exhibition in 1851 the industrial system and all that it entailed were accepted as normal. By then the overwhelming majority of the population had no direct experience of an age when life seemed to move at a more leisurely pace. But this does not of course mean that resistance to the industrial division of labour ceased altogether. On the contrary, the eventual shift to a type of economy where the majority of the labour force are employed in large organisations, with their working lives subjected to detailed direction and control, created the enduring problems of coordination and motivation – in short, the problem of *management*. The themes of conflict, control and integration within the business enterprise will recur throughout this book.

CONCLUSION

The main aim of this chapter has been to highlight the principal differences between pre-industrial, pre-capitalist societies on the one hand, and industrial capitalist societies on the other. For convenience these differences are summarised schematically in Box 3.1.

Three points need to be made about the above scheme. First, the respective features of the two types of society are *typical* features and are not mutually exclusive. That is to say, it would be totally invalid to argue that industrial capitalist societies exhibited all the characteristics on the right and none of those on the left and vice versa. For example, it would be absurd to argue that market exchange was the only form of exchange in industrial societies when personal exchanges within the family and between friends continue to play a crucial role in social life. Nonetheless it

Box 3.1 Pre-industrial and industrial society

Pre-industrial, pre-capitalist societies	**Industrial capitalist societies**
Agricultural	Industrial
Animal power	Inanimate power – machinofacture
Production for subsistence	Production for the market
Small units of production	Large units of production
Production centred on the family	Production centred on formal organisations
Personal exchange	Market exchange – the cash nexus
Village communities	Urban conurbations
Traditional religious belief	Secular ideology – the achievement ethic
Ascribed social position	Achieved social position
Dominant class: aristocracy	Dominant class: bourgeoisie
Majority class: peasantry	Majority class: proletariat
Authoritarian government	Democratic government

is the case that market transactions play a predominant role in industrial capitalist societies: most adults sell their labour for a wage which is then used to purchase most of the goods and services they need. For the typical inhabitant of a pre-capitalist society, by contrast, market transactions either do not exist or play a very minor role in social life. Accordingly we should regard these two lists of features as abstractions or stereotypes whose principal purpose is to alert us to the fundamental changes that are involved in the transition from one type of society to the other. Since they are stereotypes the extent to which societies in the real world will correspond to one or the other will be a matter of degree.

The second point is that the process of industrialisation, as will be apparent from the preceding list of features, entailed not simply changes in the economy and division of labour but broader transformations such as urbanisation, secularisation (that is, the decline of traditional religion), the emergence of democracy and of a generally more open and more mobile society. These broader changes sociologists usually group under the term 'modernisation' which refers to the social and cultural side of industrialisation. The complex interrelationship between fundamental economic change and these broader social processes will be a basic theme of this book.

Third, and most important, the mode and phasing of the transition from the pre-industrial to the industrial stage varied very significantly between the now-industrialised countries. It is neither possible nor necessary to examine even in outline the different routes to modernity taken by these countries. Suffice it to say that the British route differs quite markedly from all the others in at least three important respects. First, feudalism in Britain had withered away more than two hundred years before the 'take-off' of the Industrial Revolution during the last three decades of the eighteenth century. This meant, second, that Britain was politically unified before industrialisation. And third, Britain followed the free-market route to industrialism with the state playing only a minimal role. In most European countries (and Japan), by contrast, feudalism not only survived much longer but in many cases had to be formally abolished by governments (in France in 1793, in Germany in 1848, in Imperial Russia in 1861, in Japan in 1869). For this and other reasons political unification often coincided with rather than preceded industrialisation (this was particularly evident in Germany and Italy). And last, in all continental countries (and Japan) the state played a major pro-active role in the promotion of industrialisation. Thus although Britain was undoubtedly the first society to industrialise, the path it took seems to have differed quite radically from that followed by most of its neighbours on the Continent.

BIBLIOGRAPHY

Braudel, F. (1983) *The Wheels of Commerce* (London: William Collins).

'Capitalism', *Encyclopaedia Britannica*.

Harrison, J. F. C. (1984) *The Common People* (London: Fontana).

Hill, C. (1969) *Reformation to Industrial Revolution* (Harmondsworth: Penguin).

Postan, M. M. (1972) *Mediaeval Economy and Society* (Harmondsworth: Penguin).

Weber, M. (1976) *The Protestant Ethic and the Spirit of Capitalism* (London: Allen & Unwin).

4 Welfare Capitalism

In the year 1848 revolutionary upheavals erupted all over continental Europe. In that year Britain was to see another (as it turned out, the last) wave of Chartism – the first major industrial mass movement of protest. These upheavals, although highly diversified in terms of expression and aims, sprang from a common background of economic crisis and growing social unrest. It is therefore probably not surprising that the same year saw the publication of the *Communist Manifesto*, a political pamphlet written by Karl Marx and Friedrich Engels, which envisaged the imminent collapse of the capitalist system.

PROLETARIAN REVOLUTION

This collapse, Marx and Engels believed, would be the inevitable product of the outworking of historical laws. Central to their understanding of historical change is the idea of conflict. Conflict manifests itself in the class struggle: 'The history of all hitherto existing society is the history of the class struggle.' Thus begins the *Manifesto*. However, class conflict is itself the symptom of more deep-rooted tensions or 'contradictions' within a society, especially contradictions between the 'forces' and the 'relations' of production. By forces of production is meant a society's capacity to produce goods and services which will be a function of levels of knowledge, technological developments, the organisation of capital and labour and so forth. The relations of production are basically the relations of property, mainly which groups or classes *own* the means of production. Marx and Engels contend that, at certain stages of development, existing property relations clash with expanding productive forces. Accordingly something has to give – effectively the old set of property relations leading to the emergence of a new class system. Thus during a certain phase of the development of feudal society, feudal property relations presided over by the landed nobility came into conflict with an expanding market economy. The tangible expression of this fundamental contradiction was conflict between the feudal class and the emerging bourgeoisie. Ultimately the bourgeoisie triumphs in this struggle as it has the *economic* power to control the bulk of the production of goods and services. The centre of gravity of the economy accordingly shifts over a long period from landed to industrial interest. This transformation is usually known as a *bourgeois* revolution.

Capitalism as a system needed a dynamic commercial class, a bourgeoisie, to bring it into existence. But capitalism, particularly industrial capitalism, also required the creation of a large class of proletarians: a class of property-less wage labourers. In creating a proletariat, capitalism paradoxically produced the class that would destroy it, that would become its 'gravedigger'. Central to Marx's scenario of the collapse of capitalism is the notion that the proletariat experiences worsening living conditions. As capitalism develops, competition between businesses intensifies. Consequently survival in the market demands greater investment in industrial plant leading to a decline in profits which in turn reduces the amount that can be paid out in wages. This leads to a decline in the proletariat's standard of living. In addition the bourgeoisie, in order to maximise the productivity of labour, intensifies the rigours of the factory system. This means that working conditions deteriorate as work is reduced to sheer drudgery.

As well as producing declining living conditions for the masses, the intense competition that characterises industrial capitalism both concentrates the means of production in fewer hands – through takeovers, mergers and the like – as well as driving out those too weak to stay in the race. The *petty* bourgeoisie in particular – small businessmen, shopkeepers and so on – are increasingly forced out of business and sink into the proletariat, are 'proletarianised'. Class conflict is now polarised into a major confrontation between 'two great hostile camps': a small bourgeoisie and a vast proletariat. This conflict can only be resolved through a revolutionary uprising in which the proletariat seizes control of the means of production and the state. After passing through a transitional period comprising a form of state socialism, the communist stage of development is entered. Neither Marx nor Engels said a great deal about the actual organisation of communist society. In their writings it therefore remains a vague conception of a somewhat utopian state in which private property, the division of labour and government are abolished or 'wither away', and where man regains his essential nature as a creative animal.

For an adequate understanding of the Marxist conception of industrial society it is crucial to appreciate that although it is ultimately the actions of human beings, the proletariat, which overthrow the capitalist system, the roots of this and all other revolutions lie within the system itself. For Marx it is the system which assigns individuals to a given position within the overall division of labour and this position determines in large measure the nature of relationships with others:

in the social production of their life, men enter into definite relations that are indispensible and independent of their will, relations of production which correspond to a definite stage of development of their material productive forces. (Karl Marx, *The German Ideology*, Moscow Progress Publisher, 1976, pp. 41–2)

Thus even the proletariat's consciousness of exploitation and its source is a reflection of objective material conditions; to be specific, of the organisation of production under capitalism. Industrial capitalism is the first economic system to concentrate the bulk of the working population into large units of production. It is this concentration in factories and such like that produces an awareness among individual wage labourers that they share a common situation with their fellows. Initially such awareness will be confined to places of employment but gradually spreads to whole industries. Trade unions both express this growing consciousness and facilitate its expansion. Ultimately consciousness extends to take in the whole working class, leading to revolutionary upheaval.

The point is that the type of consciousness which develops under industrial capitalism is peculiar to it as a socioeconomic system. It could not develop, for example in pre-capitalist societies where the bulk of the population are located in small units of production, mainly family farms. Thus the overthrow of capitalism is inevitable, claims Marx, not because capitalists are greedy or the proletariat disorderly, but because this is the only way in which the system's deep-lying contradictions can be resolved.

THE 'PROBLEM' OF THE WORKING CLASS

Marx and Engel's predictions of proletarian revolution have not been validated by historical events since then. Whilst it is the case that major revolutionary upheavals have taken place this century (for example, in Mexico in 1910, in Russia in 1917, in China in 1949, in Vietnam in 1971) these have not been in mature capitalist societies where a proletariat formed the bulk of the labour force. On the contrary, these were primarily agricultural societies where the peasantry not only formed a majority but also played a pivotal role in these upheavals.

Nonetheless, it is undoubtedly the case that the new industrial system created and became dependent upon a working class, that is, a stratum of manual workers who sold their labour for a wage. By the turn of the century this working class formed an overwhelming majority of the labour force – in Britain 75 per cent in 1911. Furthermore, Marx's prediction that the concentration of the labour force in large units of production would foster collective consciousness seems to have been borne out. In every country in Western Europe the spread of industrialism has been accompanied by the expansion of the trade union movement as well as the emergence of mass left-wing parties ranging from moderate reformist (for example, the British Labour Party, German Social Democrats) to revolutionary communist. However, it needs to be emphasised that the pattern of trade union growth varied enormously between the different countries, the variations reflecting local industrial and political conditions. In Britain, for example, small exclusive craft unions were at the forefront of the movement for most of the nineteenth century. As a consequence the industrial relations scene in Britain has been characterised – plagued, some would argue – by a large number of unions (more than a thousand at the beginning of this century). In Germany, by contrast, a much greater degree of industrial concentration ('cartelisation'; see Chapter 2) had its counterpart in the formation of industrially based unions (one union for each industry) of which there were not more than 50 just before the First World War. France exhibits yet another pattern in which much lower degrees of industrial concentration have allowed the survival of a high proportion of small firms (employing 34 per cent of the labour force in 1976 as compared to 22 per cent in Britain). The greater predominance of small firms in France is thought to lie behind that country's exhibiting the lowest degree of unionisation in Western Europe (27 per cent of the labour force in 1982 as compared to 52 per cent in Britain and 50 per cent in Germany). And yet, because of the survival in French culture of a strong revolutionary strain, industrial relations there have generally been characterised by a greater militancy than in Britain or Germany.

Despite such variations there is no doubt that by the beginning of the twentieth century a European working class had emerged. Here it is crucial to emphasise that by the term 'working class' we are thinking not just of an objective statistical category but of a stratum of society which had acquired an awareness of itself in relation to other classes, most notably the property-owning bourgeoisie. This is not of course to argue that the working class in any given country was completely unified. On the contrary, like any other class it was riven by divisions, the most important of which was probably the boundary between a skilled minority – the 'labour aristocracy' – and the unskilled majority. But such divisions and variations in industrial location aside, some kind of collective consciousness, albeit fragmented, was able to assert itself and sometimes in an extremely forceful way. It needs to be understood that relations between capital and labour during the early years of this century were often extremely violent with serious injury, deaths, rioting and confrontations with the military not uncommon. Further radical and revolutionary ideas such as Marxism and Syndicalism (Box 4.1)

Box 4.1 Syndicalism

Syndicalism embodies the idea that the workers, through direct action, especially the general strike, should seize control over the means of production and hence political power. Syndicalism differs from Marxist-Leninism in that society is to be administered on a local basis through the trade unions (*syndicat* = trade union) rather than through a centralised revolutionary party. Syndicalism had little impact on Britain, its main centres of influence being France, Spain and through the IWW (Industrial Workers of the World) in the United States. Apart from in Spain, where it survived until the end of the Civil War, the appeal of syndicalism had declined significantly by the early 1920s.

---

were spreading among the working class. Whilst it is true that such ideas were never seriously embraced other than by small minorities, the mere fact of their existence was extremely alarming to employers and governments. Added to this, the Bolshevik Revolution of 1917, although not primarily a proletarian revolution, provided a vivid example of the fragility of Europe's ruling classes in the face of mass upheaval.

All this adds up to the problem of the working class, a problem which has dominated European societies for at least two-thirds of the twentieth century. That is to say, if these societies were to remain stable, this class had to be 'incorporated' in the sense of being given a much greater stake in the capitalist system. The process of incorporation was extremely complex and we can do no more here than sketch the major transformations. Suffice it to say that the capitalism that developed by the middle of the century looked radically different to that which Marx and Engels were writing about a century before. We may group these transformations under three headings: socioeconomic changes, affluence and mass democracy, and welfarism.

MAJOR SOCIOECONOMIC CHANGES DURING THIS CENTURY

For the purposes of this chapter it is proposed to highlight three major changes under this heading: the separation of ownership and control of the means of production, the emergence of the 'new middle class' and the expansion of social mobility.

Separation of ownership and control

In his later writings Marx was aware of but unable to anticipate the far-reaching consequences of the emergence of the joint-stock company: the business enterprise which raises capital by selling stocks and shares. Whilst joint-stock companies have existed for many centuries, until the late nineteenth and early twentieth centuries they were the exception rather than the rule. By the early 1960s the joint-stock company had become the dominant form of capitalist enterprise accounting for a clear majority of people employed as well as the greatest share of capital invested. This means that the enterprise owned and run by an individual or family has long ceased to be the dominant form of economic organisation.

In addition to its economic consequence it is argued that the emergence of the joint-stock company has led to a shift in the basis of the legitimacy of the firm. Whereas the old-style capitalist exercised authority through the *ownership* of property the authority of the *manager* derives from the rights delegated to him by the actual owners – the shareholders – via the board. But in addition to these delegated rights of property the manager, by virtue of his day-to-day contact with the various participants in the process of production, may need to seek a second basis of legitimacy, namely some kind of consensus involving himself and those over whom he formally exercises authority. That is to say the modern manager, unlike the owner–manager, is less able to assert his authority in an authoritarian manner which ignores the wishes and interests of his subordinates. The full implications of the separation of the ownership and control of the means of production are far-reaching and complex and will occupy our attention a good deal in later chapters. For the time being the fundamental point is that the homogenous capitalist class predicted by Marx has not developed. Whilst a capitalist class still undoubtedly survives in advanced industrial societies, executive authority within the workplace lies primarily in the hands of individuals whose legitimacy derives not from direct ownership of property but from their competition as *professional managers*. This situation is often held to affect profoundly the character of conflict in the workplace. Conflict certainly exists but seems to be a long way from the class confrontation – confrontation between a large proletariat and a small homogenous capitalist class – which Marx believed would be the principal feature of a declining capitalist society.

The 'new middle class'

When Marx died in 1883 probably less than 5 per cent of the labour force in industrial societies were in white-collar occupations. By 1960 the figure was between 35 and 40 per cent and by the end of the eighties white-collar workers were in a majority in most industrial societies. Three basic factors lie behind this expansion of the non-manual sector. First, the emergence of the large corporation required a growing army of white-collar workers – from executives to wages clerks, line managers to secretaries – to run their administrative apparatuses. Second, as we shall see below, the period following the Second World War saw a major upsurge of state involvement in Western European economies which again demanded an increase in the white-collar labour force. More civil servants, doctors, teachers, social workers and other professionals were needed by the 'welfare state'. And last it seems that as economies grow a stage is reached when the demand for services increases rapidly. This is because with higher incomes people have more money to spend on things like entertainment, holidays and personal services such as hairdressing as well as the professional services of lawyers, accountants, estate agents, psychoanalysts and so forth. Whilst by no means all employees in the service sector are non-manual (for example, motor mechanics and cleaners) it seems that the mid-century expansion there has been predominantly in the white-collar area.

The term 'new' here is meant to distinguish the salary-earning middle class – the 'salariat' – from the old-style middle class which makes its living either from profits in the case of capitalists, or from fees earned from the sale of professional services in the case of doctors, lawyers, architects and accountants. The basic problem with this concept of the new middle class is that it contains such a diversity of occupations. Post office clerks, shop assistants, typists, top civil servants and senior executives would all be included. Not surprisingly, therefore, a good deal of attention has been devoted by sociologists to trying to determine the class position of this expanding white-collar stratum. Put simply, are white-collar workers members of the bourgeoisie or the proletariat? This is an extraordinarily complex question which is impossible to resolve in this context. One's conclusion depends heavily upon which sector of the non-manual labour force is under consideration. Whilst a large proportion of white-collar workers are property-less, which makes them strictly speaking proletarians, there are very marked differences in terms of salary, status and power between, say, executives and top civil servants on the one hand, and typists and post office clerks on the other. Probably most sociologists would regard the first group as an extension of the capitalist class (bourgeoisie) whilst what are usually referred to as *routine* white-collar workers might properly be seen as part of the proletariat. But in the real world the situation is obviously much more complex. More important for the time being than the actual class position of white-collar workers is the more basic point that the evolution of this sector renders the class structure of industrial societies much more complex than Marx was able to envisage. As sociologist Ralf Dahrendorf put it in the late fifties: 'If ever there have been two large, homogeneous, polarised social classes, these have certainly ceased to exist today.'

Social mobility

Social mobility refers to movement up or down the occupational structure and is usually studied in one of two ways: either in terms of movement between generations, invariably involving a comparison of fathers' with sons' occupations; or occupational movement within a single generation. Marx was not unaware of the phenomenon of social mobility which he noted in the United States. However, Marx believed that such mobility was a feature of certain phases of historical development, primarily periods of rapid social change when new societies (like the USA in the nineteenth century) are emerging or old ones disintegrating. Marx assumed that the position an individual occupies in capitalist societies was very largely determined by family of origin, in other words, that European capitalist societies display much of the rigidity of *class closure* of their feudal predecessors. However, contemporary evidence demonstrates not only that social mobility has become an entrenched feature of industrial society, but also that its absence would endanger its very cohesion even to the point of producing breakdown. Whilst there are difficulties in interpreting the evidence it seems that rates of mobility are high in most industrialised societies. Only in the highest and in some countries in the lowest ranges of the occupational scale do we still find a considerable degree of self-recruitment. The evidence furthermore supports the notion that the educational system is more and more becoming the agency which selects individuals on the basis of ability and places them in appropriate occupations. This is not to claim the existence of a completely meritocratic society as there are still numerous obstacles to complete equality of opportunity. But it seems that there is in modern societies a tendency to establish inter-generational mobility as the norm by making a person's social position increasingly dependent upon his/her educational achievement. Furthermore, it seems that the amount of social mobility across advanced industrial societies is roughly similar. If we divide the social structure into three broad categories – working class, intermediate, and managerial and professional – the proportion of people who move from one to the other is about half, with approximately 30 per cent moving up and 20 per cent down. This would be the figure for Britain and the United States whereas for certain European countries – notably Sweden – the volume of overall mobility would be slightly higher. Despite these variations the main point is that the consequences of social mobility for the question of social stability are crucial:

where mobility both within and between generations is normal enough that most people may legitimately expect it, the intensity of social conflict may be expected to decline.

AFFLUENCE AND MASS DEMOCRACY

Most of the readers of this book will have been brought up in a world in which TV, videos, hi-fi, refrigerators, washing machines, motor cars, fitted carpets and central heating are so normal as to be unworthy of comment. Yet the consumer revolution, the 'age of high mass consumption' is a very recent development in European history. The first postwar generation was born into a world where TV was unknown, where only a small and affluent minority could afford motor cars, and where the milk always went sour in warm weather because virtually no one had refrigerators. This generation had probably left school before Prime Minister Harold Macmillan's memorable 'You've never had it so good' celebrated the arrival of the consumer eldorado. What made possible this fundamental change in the lives of Europeans, a change so profound in its consequences that a number of social commentators believed that we were entering a new and distinctive phase in the process of industrialisation? (Box 4.2)

Box 4.2 Stages of economic growth

In *The Stages of Economic Growth: A Non-Communist Manifesto* (1962) the American economist W. W. Rostow proposes a theory of economic growth (an alternative to that of Marx) based upon five stages. In the first *traditional* stage it is very difficult to expand production beyond a limited ceiling because of inadequate scientific knowledge and a traditional view which sees the world as fixed and unchangeable. Traditional societies are agrarian with rigid social structures dominated by family and clan interest. The dominant attitude is one of 'long-run fatalism' – the belief that the range of possibilities open to one's grandchildren will be just about what they were for one's grandparents.

   In the second *preconditions for take-off* stage the insights of modern science begin to be applied to agricultural and industrial production. The idea spreads that economic progress is not only possible, but desirable. New types of enterprising individual come forward who are willing to mobilise savings and take risks in the pursuit of profit. Investment increases notably in transport, communications and raw materials. But these developments proceed gradually until the threshold of the third stage, *take-off*, is reached. At this point new industries expand, rapidly yielding large profits, a considerable proportion of which are invested in new plant. Because of their expanding demand for factory workers and the goods and services to support them, these new industries stimulate the growth of others. Rostow fixes *take-off* in Britain some time in the decades after 1783; in France and the United States in the decades preceding 1860; in Germany in the third quarter of the nineteenth century; in Japan in its last quarter and in Russia and Canada during the 25 years prior to 1914. During the 1950s India and China, in their quite different ways, launched their respective take-offs. After *take-off* there follows a long interval of sustained growth as the expanding economy extends modern technology throughout the range of its activity. Between 10 and 20 per cent of national income is steadily reinvested so that output continues to outstrip increases in population. Some sixty years after *take-off* the fourth stage, the *drive to maturity*, is completed. The mature economy broadens its base to include technologically more refined and complex processes and is thus able to move beyond the industries that fuelled *take-off*. With the arrival of the fifth stage, the *age of high mass consumption*, the leading sectors of the economy shift into the manufacture of consumer goods and the provision of services. This stage can be reached only when real income per head has risen to a point at which the consumption needs of a large section of the population have moved beyond basic food, clothing and shelter. At the time when Rostow was writing (the late fifties) the *age of high mass consumption* had been reached only in North America, Western Europe and Australasia.

First, technological developments played a major role. If we look at the process of industrialisation in terms of technological evolution it is helpful to identify three phases. The first is after 1848 when the application of steam power to production became general. The second, after 1893, was marked by the diffusion of electrically powered and petrol-driven machinery. The third, which came after the Second World War, saw the general application of electronic power to the process of production. It was this third technological revolution, one which entailed the dissemination through Europe and Japan of automated and semi-automated mass-production techniques, that fuelled the postwar boom. The growth industries of the second wave – shipbuilding, coal, textiles – had gone into decline. These were in the process of being replaced by new growth industries – cars, electronics, chemicals – employing the new technology. The application of these new techniques, the enhanced *quality* of the means of production, made possible an unprecedented leap in labour productivity. By 1973 output in industrialised countries was almost three times as great as it had been in 1950. More was produced in those 25 years than in the previous 75, and many times more than at any other comparable period of human history.

But in addition to technological advance the beginning of the boom was marked by a concerted effort on the part of the industrial powers to create a stable international environment for industrial expansion and trade. A primary aim was to avoid the protectionism and currency instability that had produced the world slump in the 1930s. A crucial UN conference at Bretton Woods, New Hampshire, in 1944 attempted to set up an institutional framework which would promote economic recovery and regenerate international trade. First, Bretton Woods promoted currency convertibility through a system of stable exchange rates tied to the dollar and hence theoretically to gold. Second, Bretton Woods set up the international Monetary Fund (IMF), an international currency pool from which members might borrow in order to correct temporary deficiencies in their balance of payments. Through this type of assistance it was hoped that in the face of a trade imbalance member countries would avoid seeking a remedy in exchange controls and currency depreciation, both of which would adversely affect the flow of trade. Bretton Woods also established the International Bank for Reconstruction and Development (World Bank), whose basic role was to provide capital for long-term economic reconstruction.

Nonetheless, the resources of the Bank were limited and in fact were not equal to the task of rebuilding the economies of a Europe devastated by six years of war. Accordingly in 1947 the American Secretary of State, George Marshall, proposed a European Recovery Program aimed at the rapid regeneration of European economies. The sum of $13 billion to be spread over four years was assigned by Congress to the Program. Important though 'Marshall Aid' was in the resuscitation of industrial production in Europe it was soon to be overtaken by direct private investment by American MNCs. Between 1950 and 1970 US overseas investments generally increased from $12 billion to $78 billion. But US investments in manufacturing in Europe increased at a much faster rate from around $1 billion to $14 billion over the same 20-year period. The main attraction for this accelerating level of investment was Europe's cheap labour force and, after 1958, the opportunity to circumvent European Economic Community tariffs. The financing of such levels of investment led to massive injections of dollars into the international economy which acted as a major stimulus to international trade. Between 1951 and 1971 the volume of world trade in manufactures increased three-and-a-half-fold.

The social consequences of this tremendous increase in manufacturing capacity and trade was the radical transformation of the lives of European citizens. After a period of austerity immediately following the war European societies gradually entered, more than two decades behind the USA, the age of high mass consumption. This was an era in which a majority, now with higher disposable incomes, were able to purchase cheap mass-produced consumer goods. The expansion of the industries which produced these goods increased the demand for labour, especially skilled labour, thereby creating conditions of full employment.

However, we must bear in mind that rapid economic growth alone in no sense guarantees that the fruits of this growth will be distributed widely. As it happens the colossal expansion of industrial economies after the Second World War coincided with the consolidation of mass democracy. By the turn of the century universal male suffrage had been introduced in most European countries and as we enter the twentieth century the franchise was gradually extended to women. (In Britain, not until 1928 was the vote given to all women over 21.) But democracy is not based upon voting alone. If this were the case then the former Soviet Union, as well as many highly authoritarian states in the third world, would count as democracies. Mass democracy proper requires, first, that citizens can effectively express their needs and interests through political parties and pressure groups such as trade unions, professional or trade associations. And second, democracy requires that government be accountable for its actions. This means not simply that government (whether national or local) submit itself periodically to the verdict of the electorate, but that its actions and decisions be open to the scrutiny of the public. Accordingly, freedom of association, free and independent mass media, effective communications, as well as a literate and informed electorate, are as essential ingredients as elections and parties.

In Europe, of key significance in the development of effective mass democracy was the emergence of a strong trade union movement. This in turn eventually expressed itself in the formation of working-class parties such as the British Labour Party and the German Social Democrats as well as the various European communist parties. In fact so successful were some of these left-wing parties at winning and organising members that parties of the centre and right were forced to streamline their operations in order to meet the challenge of mass politics. The point is that since the industrial proletariat now constituted a clear majority of the electorate, parties of all political persuasions must solicit their votes. Accordingly, beginning in the last decades of the nineteenth century with newly unified Germany leading the way, we find Western governments increasingly sponsoring welfare-type legislation such as unemployment and sickness benefit. This process culminated in the emergence, after the Second World War, of a fully fledged welfare state, a development which was in no small measure a response to pressure from below.

WELFARE CAPITALISM

During the depression years of the 1930s, government thinking about the then chronically high levels of unemployment was dominated by the *laissez-faire* (Box 4.3) belief in the virtues of market forces. Unemployment was high because wages were too high (primarily because of the activities of trade unions). Let wages find their true 'market' level and the economy will move back to its natural equilibrium at full employment. Government, accordingly, should do nothing save balance its budget in the confident expectation that market forces, left to their own devices, would eventually produce a recovery.

Box 4.3 Laissez-faire

This term is understood to have originated in an exchange between the seventeenth-century French minister of finance, Jean-Baptiste Colbert, and a prominent merchant. 'What can we do for you?', Colbert is said to have asked the merchant (the 'we' referring to the French state). 'Nous laissez faire [Leave us alone]', was the merchant's reply.

Although he probably never actually used the expression '*laissez-faire*' there is no doubt that Adam Smith (1723–90), founder of modern economics, would have been in full sympathy with this sentiment. He certainly would have been strongly opposed to the wide range of protectionist measures Colbert introduced into seventeenth-century France. Whilst the regulation of industry and trade may well secure advantages for those directly affected, such arrangements are seldom of benefit to the economy as a whole:

> No regulation of commerce can increase the quantity of industry in any society beyond what its capital can maintain. It can only divert a part of it into a direction into which it might not otherwise have gone; and it is by no means certain that this artificial direction is likely to be more advantageous to the society than that into which it would have gone of its own accord ... (*The Wealth of Nations*, Book IV, ch. 2)

Accordingly, Smith strongly advocated that government intervention in the economy be kept to a minimum, effectively confined to those areas which were unlikely to attract private investment because they were insufficiently profitable. The provision of a judicial system, a standing army, and certain public works such as highways, bridges, canals and harbours are examples of areas where governments would probably need to step in. Smith also conceded that the state would have to provide 'institutions for promoting the instruction of the people', in other words a system of public education.

In 1936 this position came under serious attack from economist John Maynard Keynes (1883–1946) who in his *General Theory* argued forcefully against the cuts in public spending that a balanced budget had required. Such cuts, by reducing the level of demand in the economy, would simply exacerbate the level of unemployment and so further deepen the recession. What government should be doing, insisted Keynes, was to *increase* its spending. By pumping money into the economy the level of demand would be raised and the recessionary spiral broken.

However, Keynes's ideas were heretical to the Treasury mandarins of the thirties primarily because he questioned the fundamental orthodoxy that the market is a self-regulating mechanism. It took the Second World War and the widespread government intervention that it demanded to jerk the British economy out of recession and in the process persuade statesmen and policy-makers that Keynes was, after all, basically right. The end of the war inaugurated the 'Keynesian Era', a 30-year period during which successive governments employed Keynesian 'demand management' strategies in their attempts to maintain full employment.

In addition to demand management the postwar British government assumed direct ownership and control of certain areas of the economy: notably coal, steel, gas and electricity production and road and rail transport. Whilst there were valid economic arguments for these nationalisations there was also a strong ideological element. The 1945 General Election had resulted in a landslide victory for the British Labour Party in whose socialist scenario nationalisation played a prominent role. Nationalisation was seen as a means of fundamentally altering the pattern of ownership and control of industry and through this the distribution of wealth and power in the economy and in society.

Equally important the Labour Government also set up a comprehensive welfare system which included a compulsory scheme of national insurance for unemployment and sickness benefits, retirement pensions, family allowances, maternity and death grants and a non-contributory National Health Service. The government also made subsidies available for the building of council houses and the creation of new towns which could cater for the rehousing needs of London and other large cities. These reforms were in line with the recommendations of the Beveridge Report, which had become a bestseller in 1942, and which aimed to set up a welfare support system which covered the complete life-span – 'from the cradle to the grave'. It is crucial to understand that the welfare state, although to a considerable extent the outcome of a tide of popular support for the Labour Party, once established, was not dismantled by the Conservative Government when it came to power in 1951. Furthermore, although the Tories denationalised steel and road transport, the fundamentals of the mixed economy were retained as was the commitment to full employment. 'Party differences', stated Conservative Prime Minister Winston Churchill in 1953, 'are now in practice mainly those of emphasis.' As a consequence Britain enjoyed high levels of employment for at least 30 years from 1942 until the mid-seventies. Only in the second half of the seventies, with the onset of the world recession, did unemployment begin to rise from 2.5 per cent or under to 5 per cent and above.

A combination of welfarism, full employment and the postwar boom led to a steady increase in the standard of living of a majority of the population. The average earnings of manual workers rose from the equivalent of £31 in 1951 (at 1975 prices) to £54 in 1975. Those whose standards had previously been the lowest, the semi-skilled and the unskilled, benefited the most; clerical and salary-earners the least. Much of the extra income was spent on private housing, furniture and domestic equipment. By 1961 three out of four houses had a vacuum cleaner, two out of five a washing machine and one in three a refrigerator. Four out of five had a TV set with the number of licences doubling between 1955 and 1959 alone. Nearly all of these 'luxuries', as they were then regarded, were bought with the aid of credit, Britain's hire purchase debt doubling between 1955 and 1961. The late fifties inaugurated the age of the motor car with the completion of Britain's first motorway and the introduction of parking meters. The significance of the arrival of the 'age of affluence' cannot be overstated: relative freedom from fear of unemployment, illness and old age, as well as an income above the level of basic necessities, was something entirely new for the overwhelming majority of working people.

The attainment of high levels of affluence and welfare provision was by no means confined to Britain, having become by the early sixties the norm virtually throughout Western Europe (with exceptions on the European periphery such as Eire, Portugal, southern Spain, southern Italy and Greece). The principal factors behind the development of welfare capitalism were, first, pressure from below embodying a widespread expectation, provoked by wartime deprivation, of a better life, and second, the need of governments to rebuild war-shattered economies and restore productive capacity. The onset of the Cold War and the perceived threat of communism gave added urgency to this task and made a return to the stagnation and mass unemployment of the thirties impossible. The postwar boom in the world economy enabled capitalism to be managed along Keynesian lines to such a degree that a number of commentators believed that the system's basic defects (most apparent during the thirties) had finally been overcome. Hence Labour Member of Parliament and theoretician of a revised form of socialism Anthony Crosland could claim in 1956: 'Traditionally, or at least since Marx, socialist thought has been dominated by the economic problems posed by capitalism, poverty, mass unemployment, squalor and even the possibility of the collapse of the whole system... Capitalism has been reformed out of all recognition. Despite occasional minor recessions and balance of payments crises, full employment and at least a tolerable degree of stability are likely to be maintained' (*The Future of Socialism*).

AFFLUENCE AND THE CLASS STRUCTURE

By the sixties a number of sociologists too had come round to the view that modern capitalist society had been able to resolve the fundamental tensions with which it had hitherto been afflicted. Indeed for certain writers the term 'capitalism' was increasingly inappropriate, the key variable being *industrialism*. Industrial Society was seen as a fundamental type with capitalism being but one way of organising industrialism. The keynote of this Industrial Society is scientific rationality, that is to say, the application of scientific thinking not only to production and to the organisation of the firm, but to society in general. The emphasis is therefore upon planning, the planning of production, of education, communications, municipal and social services, of social relations generally. The Industrial Society perspective embodies a confidence in the power of human reason, in the effectiveness of public planning. Thus whilst tensions and conflict are bound to develop it is possible to establish institutional arrangements which are capable of resolving them. Negotiating committees, arbitration boards and other mechanisms of conciliation ensure that grievances can be aired and differences resolved. Conflict is therefore restricted to the local level, usually to the firm or industry where it breaks out. The idea of *class* conflict, conflict which transcends local and specific interests, is largely obsolete. Indeed there is serious doubt whether in this perspective, classes themselves continue to exist. Certainly the problematical working class of the Marxists seems to have disappeared, to have been absorbed into a huge amorphous middle class. 'The dominant picture of John Bull puts him in the solid middle class suburban range', claimed a British government report in 1962. This process of '*embourgeoisement*' (becoming bourgeois, that is, middle class) was by no means confined to Britain. A phenomenon of all developed capitalist societies, it was supposedly the inevitable outcome of a number of interrelated economic, social and technological changes. First, economic growth had resulted in a significant increase in working-class incomes and ownership of consumer goods. Second, the welfare commitment to improving housing standards had led to the re-development of inner-city slum areas and in many cases to the relocation of the working class to the suburbs and new towns. Third, technological developments had transformed the labour process so that manual labour was now less likely to involve hard physical toil and more likely to entail the superintendance of machines.

Since it was first proposed in the late fifties and early sixties, the *embourgeoisement* argument has been subjected to a good deal of critical scrutiny. In one of the best-known studies carried out in Luton in the mid-sixties, J. H. Goldthorpe and his collaborators concluded that as it stands the thesis is to be rejected.

The key question to which Goldthorpe *et al.* address themselves is whether affluence by itself is indicative of middle-class status? They argue that it is not and that for *embourgeoisement* proper to take place discernible movement along three dimensions is necessary: the *economic*, the *normative* and the *relational*. That is to say, manual workers must be shown to be earning middle-class incomes; second, there should be evidence that these manual workers identify with the middle class and are adopting its norms; and, third, manual workers should regularly mix socially with people of middle-class status.

After interviewing samples of both manual and non-manual workers in the Luton area Goldthorpe concludes that *embourgeoisement* is not taking place. In terms of the *economic* dimension it was the case that their manual workers were earning as much and sometimes more than routine non-manual workers. However, it is important to note that relatively high manual earnings were achieved only as a result of considerable amounts of overtime and shift-working. Second, there was no evidence of the wide-spread adoption of middle-class *norms*. Two-thirds of their manual workers clearly identified themselves with the working class and there was also majority support for trade unions and the Labour Party. Neither was there, in terms of the *relational* dimension, much evidence of mixing with the middle classes or the adoption of middle-class patterns of sociability such as dining out. Leisure patterns tended to conform to those of the traditional working class (Box 4.4) with recreation not passed with the immediate family being spent mainly with relatives.

However, it is crucial to note that, although rejecting the *embourgeoisement* argument, Goldthorpe *et al.* are not insisting that the working class has not changed. The affluent manual worker, they maintain, differs from his more traditional counterpart in at least two important and related respects. First, his allegiance to trade unions and the Labour Party is much more pragmatic, based on a fairly clearheaded assessment of the benefits his support is likely to bring him. This '*instrumental* collectivism' contrasts with the much more deep-rooted and generally unquestioning commitment to these institutions of the proletarian. And, second, the affluent worker is much more involved with the nuclear family and the home, is more 'home-centred' than the traditional proletarian. For this reason Goldthorpe *et al.* refer to him as the *privatised* worker, meaning that his primary interests and preoccupations lie in the private sphere of home and family.

Box 4.4 The traditional working class

According to a number of sociologists and social historians, the last decades of the nineteenth century saw the emergence in Britain and Europe of a distinct pattern of working-class living together with a working-class view of the world or culture. This way of life was based upon more or less homogeneous communities of manual workers living in close proximity and with a high degree of social interaction between workmates, family, friends and neighbours (what in the sociological literature are termed *integrated occupational communities*). Such communities were the outcome of a distinct pattern of growth during the early stages of industrialisation when core industries such as coal, textiles, engineering and shipbuilding needed large volumes of labour. In an age before extensive commuting networks, this labour force needed to be housed close to the factories, mines or shipyards. Consequently, in areas where such industries developed, large numbers of people worked together, lived together, spent their leisure together, befriended and married each other. The strong solidarity which springs from such proximity expressed itself politically in fervent support for trade unions and for left-wing parties such as the British Labour Party, the German Social Democrats and, in France and Italy, the Communist Party. The 'traditional proletarian', as he has been termed, tended to subscribe to a 'them and us' view of the world. 'They', the bosses, the ruling class, have the power to exploit 'us' and there is little we can do to change the situation. We can, however, use our numbers to stick together and defend our living standards against attacks by the employers. This 'sticking together' through trade unionism and industrial militancy, for example, has been referred to as 'solidaristic collectivism'. This does not of course mean that all manual workers in traditional 'smokestack' industries subscribed to this working-class view of the world. As we would expect there were substantial variations in outlook in the same industry in different countries. Miners, for example, were until recently the very embodiment of working-class solidarity in Britain whereas in France they were slow to unionise and have tended to remain at the periphery of the labour movement. Again within the same industry in one country there might be differences of outlook by region or level of skill. In relation to the latter, skilled workers in most of Europe have tended to consider themselves to some extent as apart from the rest of the manual sector even to the extent of sometimes seeing themselves as a separate class. But despite this variation it is still useful to talk of a working-class view of the world, one that places a heavy emphasis on solidarity and collectivism. This contrasts sharply with the middle-class emphasis on individualism – getting on solely through one's own efforts. (Two of the best-known English community studies are M. Young and P. Wilmott (1962) *Family and Kinship in East London* and N. Dennis *et al.* (1957) *Coal is our Life*. See also T. Zeldin (1979) *France 1848–1945: Ambition and Love*.)

The first point to make about these observations is that the prediction about the emergence of a more pragmatic approach to politics and unionism, so far as Britain is concerned, has been borne out by election results during the eighties and nineties. These have revealed a dramatic decline in manual support for the Labour Party from 60 per cent (voting Labour) in the sixties to less than 40 per cent in the eighties. More generally, whilst it is undoubtedly the case that manual workers currently enjoy levels of consumption that are probably not vastly different from a significant proportion of the non-manual sector, this does not entitle us to talk glibly about *embourgeoisement*. Goldthorpe's point about high manual earnings being heavily dependent upon overtime and shift-working (which makes them very vulnerable to market changes) is a very important one. There is no doubt that the further we move into the twentieth century the more hazy the manual/non-manual boundary – never rigidly demarcated – becomes. Nonetheless, it is still the case that throughout the industrialised world manual workers generally earn less than non-manuals, are less likely to enjoy fringe benefits such as sick pay and pension rights, are more likely to work in dirty and dangerous surroundings and to suffer injury or death as well as endure unemployment more frequently.

RECESSION

For many the basic weakness of Keynesian demand management is that it requires large injections of money into the economy. Throughout the sixties government expenditure in Western Europe grew faster than GDP. That is to say, a larger and larger proportion of GDP passed into the hands of state agencies as governments sought to regulate their economies in order to maintain the level of demand and hence sustain improvements in living standards. This excessively high supply of money, for a number of economists and politicians, was deemed to be the primary cause of inflation. In addition high levels of state expenditure were held to place an intolerable burden on the private sector. And so far as Britain was concerned, the performance of the private sector left a good deal to be desired.

The popular explanation for this poor performance attributed blame firmly to the trade union movement. Under conditions of full employment the unions were able to use or 'abuse' their power to push up wages without corresponding rises in productivity. This problem was supposed to be part-icularly acute in the strongly unionised but 'unproductive' public sector. Whether in fact industrial relations in Britain were worse than in other industrial countries, that striking is a peculiarly 'British disease', is a matter of some dispute. Nonetheless it cannot be denied that the number of working days lost through strikes in Britain in the 1970s showed a more than threefold increase over the figure for the sixties. Faced with declining profits due to more intense competition and rising labour costs, the large corporations which, since the merger boom of the sixties, now dominated the British industrial scene, behaved in a truly oligopolistic style and increased their prices. The now well-entrenched inflationary spiral was given a further twist by the oil price hikes in 1973/74 (fourfold increase) and 1979 (more than doubled). The 1974 increase launched a world reces-sion, creating chronic balance of payments difficulties for LDCs, drastic-ally reducing their capacity to import and consequently producing a sharp decline in the growth rates of the industrial economies. The year 1976 saw a partial recovery at least of the stronger economies – Japan, Germany and the United States – but the 1979 increase ushered in a second recession which, although shallower than that which came after 1974, proved to be longer-lasting. This durability stems from the deliberate adoption by the governments of the industrialised world of tight monetary policies in an attempt to bring down inflation. As a result unemployment, which climbed to around 5 per cent during the first recession, after 1979 exceeded 8 per cent in industrial capitalist economies generally. In Britain, where since 1979 monetarist policies have been pursued with uncompromising vigour, unemployment in the eighties topped 11 per cent, more than twice the highest figure for the seventies (4.8 per cent in 1977).

CONCLUSION

It was suggested at the beginning of this chapter that the development of industrial capitalism created the problem of the working class. That is to say, the industrial system in its earlier stages required a huge army of manual wage labourers. Since many of these were concentrated in large factories and in towns and cities, some kind of collective conscious-ness began to emerge. Whilst it would obviously be simplistic to term this consciousness 'revolutionary', the European working class was sufficiently volatile to be perceived by the ruling class as a threat to the established order. In the interests of long-term stability this was a class which had to be incorporated into, in the sense of given a stake in, the capitalist system. By the middle of the twentieth century, however, it seemed that economic growth and the prosperity it made possible, together with Keynesian economic policies, had permitted a considerable degree of incorporation. A number of writers including sociologists came round to the view that Industrial Society – supposedly a distinctive stage in socio-economic development – had resolved the fundamental problem of destabilising class conflict. However, as the sixties wore into the seventies it became apparent that the Industrial Society perspective had taken an overly optimistic view of social evolution. Recession and stagflation (high inflation with low growth) produced a strong reaction against Keynesianism and indeed a return to the very *laissez-faire* outlook of which Keynes had been so critical. The abandonment of the commitment to full employment, together with the swingeing cuts in public expenditure that were required by the determination to 'roll back the state', heralded a new era in the organisation of work. For many writers the nature of the transformation of work in the late twentieth century has been so far-reaching as to suggest that the industrialised world is entering a radically new stage of development. However in order to understand the full implications of the changes going on around us we will need to look in some detail at the development of the large corporation, of management and of the formal organisation of work under capitalism.

BIBLIOGRAPHY

Abercrombie, N. et al. (1988) *Contemporary British Society* (Oxford: Polity Press).
Armstrong, P., Glyn, A. and Harrison, J. (1984) *Capitalism Since World War II* (London: Fontana).
Coates, D. (1984) *The Context of British Politics* (London: Hutchinson).
Dahrendorf, R. (1963) *Class and Class Conflict in Industrial Societies* (London: Routledge & Kegan Paul).
Dennis, N. et al. (1957) *Coal is Our Life* (London: Eyre & Spottiswood).
Giddens, A. (1980) *The Class Structure of Advanced Societies* (London: Hutchinson).
Goldthorpe, J. H. (1966) 'Attitudes and Behaviour of Car Assembly Workers', *British Journal of Sociology*, vol. 17.
Goldthorpe, J. H., Lockwood, D., Bechhofer, F. and Platt, J. (1969) *The Affluent Worker in the Class Structure* (Cambridge: Cambridge University Press).
Kerr, C., Dunlop, J. T., Harbison, F. and Myers, C. A. (1973) *Industrialism and Industrial Man* (Harmondsworth : Penguin).

Welfare Capitalism   69

Marx, K. and Engels, F. (1967) *The Communist Manifesto* (London: Methuen).
Rider, J. and Silver, H. (1977) *Modern English Society* (London: Methuen).
Rostow, W. W. (1962) *The Stages of Economic Growth: A Non-Communist Manifesto* (Cambridge: Cambridge University Press).
Skildelsky, R. (ed.) (1978) *The End of the Keynesian Era* (London: Macmillan).
Young, M. and Wilmott, P. (1962) *Family and Kinship in East London* (Harmondsworth; Penguin).
Zeldin, T. (1979) *France 1848–1945. Ambition and Love* (Oxford: Oxford University Press).

5 Corporations and Managers

The most outstanding feature of the economic enterprise in the pre-industrial era is the close interdependency between the family on the one hand and economic activities on the other. This interdependency is most apparent in the case of the peasant farm which produces for its own consumption and is organised around the patriarchal family. That is to say, family members work under the direction of the patriarchal head and the principles of kinship, backed by tradition and custom, determine who does what and how, as well as what each is entitled to receive in return. Family members under this system are not *paid* in the modern sense of receiving wages but get back *in kind* – food, a place to live, access to land and to the labour of others – some customarily laid-down equivalent for their efforts. In fact not only are family and economic roles closely interlinked but more generally one's position in a given kinship group tends to determine the character of social relationships in all areas of social life: not only whom you work with and how labour is performed, but whom you associate closely with, befriend, spend your leisure with, marry, worship with and can look to for support of various kinds. The process of development and modernisation is essentially one in which family roles become separated or *differentiated* from other social and economic roles.

Peasant agriculture always exists in an interdependent relationship, with towns and cities supplying agricultural commodities – both foodstuffs and raw materials – which are then transformed into commodities for sale – bread, beer, cloth and the like. Towns and cities, in other words, imply trade and commerce, in short a cash economy. But although the craftsman of the pre-modern era (say England in the sixteenth century) is integrated into a cash economy, the basic unit of production continues to be centred upon the family. Production takes place in the home, is organised around family members with additional help from living-in apprentices as well as, during busy periods, other relatives and neighbours. This form of enterprise whose nucleus rested in the family, persisted well into the industrial era and has by no means disappeared. Nor is it confined to the small craft work-shop, adjoining or tacked on to living accommodation. Whilst business may have been conducted away from the home (that is, work had become differentiated from the domestic sphere) in large trading ventures and early factories, family relationships continued to supply the main principles of organisation until long after the Industrial Revolution. Clark Kerr and his associates have used the term *patrimonial* management to denote the situ-

70

ation where family and other personal relationships form the core of the business enterprise, that is, where ownership and overall day-to-day direction are clearly in the hands of a single family or group of families. Kerr sees patrimonial management as typical of the early stages of capitalist development. However, as firms increase in size it becomes more and more difficult for a single family or alliance of families to provide recruits for all 'managerial' positions. Increasingly the family must cede control to qualified outsiders, that is to managers. The emergence of the manager and its corollary, the growth in the size of the industrial enterprise, the appearance, that is, of the large corporation, is one of the most significant and far-reaching developments in the evolution of capitalism. It is a development that appears to signify a fundamental change in the basic character of the firm from an enterprise run by the propertied capitalist on the one hand, to the corporation, the *joint-stock company* (see Box 5.1) presided over by property-less managers on the other. Before examining the social consequences of this transformation let us first look briefly at the process of industrial concentration that underlies it.

Box 5.1 The joint-stock company

A joint-stock company is an organisation of individuals who contribute money to a common stock of capital which is then employed in some branch of trade or business. The contributors proceed to share in the profit or loss that arises therefrom. A form of joint-stock company was to be found in the ancient world and arose out of the need to finance trading ventures and spread risks. Typically, however, such companies existed only for the duration of a particular voyage after which they would be dissolved. The organisation of such companies on a permanent basis is bound up with the commercial revolution of the sixteenth century. The East India Company (1600) and the Dutch East India Company (1602) were the modern joint-stock companies' prototypes. The subsequent expansion in trade and commerce resulted in the rapid proliferation of this form of organisation. However, so far as England was concerned, most of the companies were technically illegal since they had been set up without the necessary authority of a royal charter. This meant that their investors were not protected by limited liability. After a great wave of speculation ruined a large number of people in 1719, the Bubble Act was passed, making it illegal to form a company without a charter. In fact this piece of legislation proved to be a brake on the mobilisation of capital and hence on economic development. The large amounts of capital needed for canal construction in the second half of the eighteenth century demanded a simplification of the system so that towards the end of the century royal charter was superseded by Act of Parliament as the means of setting up a joint-stock company. But this was still an expensive and elaborate process, a serious impediment to business activities especially after 1840 when huge amounts of capital were needed to finance the building of the railways. Accordingly a series of Acts in the

1840s and 1850s greatly simplified the process, enabling a company to be set up under a system of registration. The Limited Liability Act of 1855 made limited liability generally available, which meant that investors in what was registered as a limited company were only liable, in the event of failure, for the amount of their investment. Unlimited liability (which still exists) means quite literally that one's liability is unlimited to the extent that one might have to sell one's house, car and other goods and chattels to meet commercial debts. Clearly the general availability of limited liability removed a major disincentive to risking one's capital. But despite this and other legislative changes the family business remained the characteristic form of enterprise in Britain until the First World War. Family businesses continue to predominate in certain areas of the economy, notably agriculture, construction, retailing and services generally (although, as we shall see below, these latter two areas are increasingly being penetrated by large conglomerates). In Europe family-based firms, in manufacturing as well as services, seem to have had a better survival rate than in Britain.

INDUSTRIAL CONCENTRATION

The driving force behind the Industrial Revolution was the entrepreneur – people like Richard Arkwright, Josiah Wedgwood and Robert Owen – who brought together capital and labour to produce goods for profit and in the process contributed to phenomenal economic expansion. The early years of industrialisation were dominated by the owner–manager, the businessman who, as well as putting up the capital for his enterprise, took a major active role in its day-to-day operation. As the scale of production expanded, particularly with the dawn of the railway age, the capital needs of industry increased. But even after the introduction of limited liability in 1855, the joint-stock company was slow to get off the ground in Britain. By 1855 limited companies accounted for at the most 10 per cent of business organisations in Britain. Throughout the nineteenth century the basic device for bringing more capital into an enterprise was to take in additional partners. Towards the end of the century a number of mergers took place in certain industries – mainly textiles, iron and steel, cement and tobacco. But new giants like the Calico Printers' Association and Associated Portland Cement were at this stage not modern centrally managed corporations, rather agglomerations of a large number of traditional family firms. The era of the modern corporation in Britain did not dawn until after the First World War.

The twenties and thirties were a period during which Britain moved from the position of being the least to one of the most concentrated economies.

As we would expect this shift can be related to international economic conditions. The world recession triggered by the Wall Street collapse of 1929 placed a premium on cost-cutting and efficiency. Faced with the example of large streamlined American corporations, British industrialists sought economies of scale through the adoption of the corporate model. In 1914 Britain's industrial structure was dominated by many thousands of small specialised family-financed and family-operated firms. During the twenties and thirties, in one industry after another, the family firm gradually gave way to the registered company owned by thousands, possibly tens of thousands, of shareholders and run by its elected board of directors. Even by 1935 half of the labour force was working in firms employing more than 500. The prewar trend towards concentration greatly accelerated after 1945 and especially during the fifties and sixties. Between 1950 and 1973 an astonishing 9538 firms disappeared as a result of mergers. Half of these went between 1960 and 1969, encouraged by a government policy expressly directed at fostering large-scale business organisation. The giant firm has now become typical for manufacturing industries. By 1972 45 per cent of manufacturing employees worked in establishments of 5000 or more, and 60 per cent in those employing 500 or more. But the trend is not confined to manufacturing: in service industries – banking, insurance, retail distribution and catering especially – large organisations have made substantial headway. Overall only slightly more than 20 per cent of the labour force now work in small businesses (that is, less than 200 employees).

Concentration has also transformed the character of competition in many industries. Large-scale organisation does not of itself produce monopolistic tendencies. Mere growth in the size of firms need not restrict competition. Furthermore, firms which increased the scale of their operations were not driven initially by the desire for the monopolistic control of markets. The primary factors behind expansion were the economic advantages of size encouraged by major advances in office technology and administrative techniques. The emergence of new mass consumer markets and the efficient means of transport to supply them also fostered *mass* production in large units. Nonetheless, growing concentration in Britain was certainly associated with the restriction of competition. By 1930 several industries – chemicals, soap, margarine manufacture, whisky-distilling, the manufacture of matches, glass bottles and yeast – were dominated by a single firm controlling as much as 70 per cent of capacity in that industry. So persistent was the tendency towards monopoly in the thirties that in 1937 a contemporary observer felt able to claim: 'As a feature of industrial and commercial organisation free competition has nearly disappeared from the British scene' (quoted by Sidney Pollard (1934) *The Development of the British Economy*).

The internationalisation of production and the emergence of the multinational corporation has accelerated the drift towards monopoly. Before the First World War the number of genuine international firms was very small but since 1918 and especially since 1945 there has been a significant increase in the export of productive capital as firms have entered into production outside their national territories. These MNCs are no longer confined to infrastructure (ports, railways) and extraction (mines, quarrying, oil), their traditional areas of penetration, but now dominate the entire manufacturing sector (engineering, petrochemicals, pharmaceuticals, food processing, papermaking and printing) and are increasingly moving into services (banking, tourism, advertising). The arrival of foreign investment in the United Kingdom on a significant scale in the sixties greatly reinforced existing tendencies towards monopoly by obliging British firms in certain industries to merge. By means of this tactic they hoped to meet foreign competition by rationalising their operations. The competition came initially from large and extremely well-organised American corporations which in the early sixties accounted for three-quarters of foreign investment in Britain. Latterly, Japanese and Western European MNCs have expanded their presence in Britain's corporate sector. Multinational corporations, as we saw in Chapter 2, are overwhelmingly monopolistic or oligopolistic in character, engaging in what is usually termed 'non-price competition'. Recognising that unrestrained price competition in an industry dominated by a few giants would be mutually destructive, such firms compete by attempting to enlarge their share of the market by means of sophisticated marketing strategies, product differentiation, brand identification and, where possible, taking over their rivals.

The United States, as already suggested, exhibits a quite different pattern of development. Whilst American industrialisation, like that of Britain and most other European countries, began with many small and medium-sized family firms, the shift into the corporate era was much more rapid. This parallels America's phenomenal rate of expansion with industrial output tripling between 1877 and 1892. From being a predominantly agrarian society in the 1840s the United States had become by 1890 the world's major industrial power. A wave of mergers in the last two decades of the nineteenth century established many industries on a firm oligopolistic basis. Between 1896 and 1905 alone the hundred largest American corporations quadrupled in size. In 1870 a factory employing more than 500 was the exception. By 1900 there were at least 1500 plants of this size, a third of them employing more than a thousand people. This was an era of extremely ruthless competition, an age during which American business heroes such as Andrew Carnegie and John D. Rockefeller bent their energies mercilessly to undercut and drive out their opponents in the production of steel, oil and the manufacture of agricultural machinery. Consequently at least half a century before Europe much of American industry was firmly set in the oligopolistic mould with domination by a small number of giant corporations.

Leading Western European countries, by contrast, seem to exhibit much lower degrees of concentration than both the United States and Britain. If we look at manufacturing, the spread of mass-production techniques particularly after the Second World War is usually associated with a high level of concentration. This indeed appears to be the case if we take the example of Britain where in 1976 only 23 per cent of the labour force was employed in small firms. However, if we turn to consider continental Europe we find the figure is as high as 52 per cent in Denmark (1973), 47 per cent in Italy (1971) and even (the then) West Germany, a world leader in manufactured goods, had 37 per cent of its manufacturing labour force in small firms in 1970. It thus seems that in this respect Britain is something of an exception. Why this is the case is bound up with complex historical reasons which cannot be explored here. Suffice it to say that despite these variations there can be little doubt that the trend towards industrial concentration (in all sectors) continues apace as the sinews of the world economy are drawn closer together. However, this does not prefigure the demise of the small firm. On the contrary, as we approach the end of this century, a number of factors, mainly economic and technological, may be combining to breathe new life into the small enterprise. This argument we will look at towards the end of this chapter. Let us first consider the major social consequences of the development of the large corporation: the emergence of formal organisation and management.

FORMAL ORGANISATION

Whatever the pattern of ownership – whether concentrated in the hands of a few individuals or families or dispersed – once a certain size is reached the more complex a firm's organisation must become. In the small firm, relationships between owner – manager and employees and amongst the latter are likely to be face-to-face, that is, communication will be by word of mouth and working methods flexible. But once we move beyond a certain scale, especially when we are dealing with thousands of employees, communications will become more and more impersonal and working methods will be governed by standardised rules and procedures. In other words the firm will acquire more and more of the trappings of *formal* organisation.

Formal organisation has been defined as 'the planned co-ordination of the activities of a number of people for the achievement of some common, explicit purpose or goal, through division of labour and function, and through a hierarchy of authority and responsibility' (E. H. Schein, *Organizational Psychology*, 1988). Goals, division of labour and function, and hierarchy are, then, the principal features of formal organisations. These are the features embodied in Max Weber's ideal type of rational-legal bureaucracy (Box 5.2). Writing at the turn of the century Weber discerned a growing tendency in industrial societies for more and more areas of social life to be patterned along bureaucratic lines. This was most apparent in the field of government and the economy but was by no means confined to these areas. Voluntary associations such as political parties and churches tended increasingly to approximate to the ideal type.

Box 5.2 Max Weber's ideal type of modern bureaucracy

Principal features
1. Incumbents are personally free and subject to the authority inherent in the bureaucracy (whether a firm, department of state, trade union or whatever) only with respect to their impersonal official obligations. In other words this authority does not apply to other spheres of life, for example family, recreation, and so on.
2. Incumbents are organised in a clearly defined hierarchy of positions or statuses.
3. Each position has a clearly defined sphere of competence.
4. The position is filled on the basis of a free contractual relationship.
5. Candidates are selected according to rational and, in principle, objective criteria such as formal qualifications and performance assessments.
6. Employees are remunerated by fixed salaries in money with the salary graded according to rank. Incumbency usually entails pension rights.
7. The position is treated as the sole or, at least, primary occupation of the incumbent.
8. Employment entails the notion of a 'career' with promotion based upon objective criteria such as seniority or achievement.
9. There is a strict separation between the incumbent and the office in the sense that the latter and everything that does with it are the property of the specific organisation and therefore cannot be appropriated for personal use.
10. Incumbents are subjected to a strict and impartial system of discipline.

It cannot be emphasised too strongly that the above features combine into a *pure* type or model to which bureaucracies in the real world will merely *approximate*. In formulating his ideal type of modern bureaucracy Weber was thinking of the contrast with pre-modern or *patrimonial* bureaucracies. In a patrimonial bureaucracy 'officials' are usually kin, clients, dependants of the head or even slaves, and are therefore not free in the modern sense of the term. Officials are selected on the basis of kinship ties, favouritism, patronage, political expediency or other subjective criteria. They are seldom paid a salary but are permitted to appropriate a portion of what is administered, for example, taxes, customs duties. A patrimonial bureaucracy coheres around *personal* needs and interests whereas modern bureaucracy is based upon *impersonal* (that is, rational-legal) principles, for example, articles of association, written constitutions, contracts.

Source: Principal characteristics adapted from Max Weber (1964) *The Theory of Social and Economic Organisation* (London: The Free Press).

In using this particular ideal type Weber is simply suggesting that in the real world some organisations will be more bureaucratic than others. This has been demonstrated very effectively by Derek Pugh and his colleagues at the University of Aston in a series of studies carried out in the sixties. What is especially interesting about the 'Aston School's' research is that it breaks down formal organisation into the following components:

(i) *Specialisation* which refers to the extent to which the functions of public relations, advertising, sales, purchasing, research and development, personnel and market research are represented by separate departments.

(ii) *Standardisation* which signifies the extent to which recruitment, training, job descriptions, working practices and discipline are standardised.

(iii) *Formalisation* which refers to the extent to which rules, procedures and the other items under (ii) are written down in handbooks, manuals, standing orders, minutes of meetings, and so forth.

(iv) *Centralisation* which is concerned with the issue of how far respective decisions must be referred up the hierarchy before action can be taken.

(v) *Configuration* which refers to the span of authority, that is, how many people work under authority figures from the chief executive down to foremen. Basically configuration is about the *shape* of an organisation. An organisation with a narrow span of authority will be tall and thin whereas one with a wide span will be short and fat.

Using these five dimensions the Aston researchers went on to study 47 organisations in public services, manufacturing and retailing. By scoring every one of the organisations along the various dimensions they were able to derive a profile of each. The profile represents the degree to which that organisation is formally structured. One of the main findings of the research corroborates Weber's view that the overall degree of formalisation is determined primarily by size: the larger an organisation the more bureau-cratic its structure. This means that its employees are more likely to work in specialised areas, following standardised procedures subject to forma-lised documentation. In a small firm, by contrast, there will be a much greater degree of flexibility: the boss may have to do his/her own market research and advertising as well as look after sales. He/she will usually take charge of such research and development as exists, probably assisted by the foreman. The foreman, in addition to fulfilling his/her normal supervisory role, will probably have to look after training as well as making sure that the firm's vehicles are regularly serviced. The boss's secretary may also act as receptionist as well as helping out with the odd sales drive. Communica-tions in the small firm will tend to be by word of mouth rather than through memos and other formal procedures.

MANAGERS

Joint-stock companies raise capital by selling shares to the public whether as individuals or in the form of other corporate organisations such as investment companies, trusts and so forth. The capital raised is used to finance the commercial operations of the company in question: to buy raw materials and equipment; to pay for salaries, advertising and marketing; to fund research and development and suchlike. Shareholders hope to earn a dividend on their investment, this dividend being determined ultimately by the profit the company makes in any given year. The overall conduct of company affairs is supervised by its board which will be made up of both executive and non-executive directors. The latter do not take part in the day-to-day running of the enterprise but are there to represent the interests of the shareholders often as major investors themselves, or because as, say, accountants or directors of other companies, they have particular expertise. Executive directors, by contrast, whilst participating in the general direc-tion of the company, also have specific responsibility for running some area of day-to-day activity, for example, purchasing, production, accounts, sales. They are the firm's managers and are paid a salary for their services. These executive managers (as well as other managers) may well be share-holders. However, the key point is that their authority within the corpora-tion and in relation to shareholders in general derives primarily from their expertise as managers, that is, from their qualifications, experience and on-the-job performance.

But what do we mean by the term 'management'? A recent definition designates it as 'the process of planning, organising, directing and controlling the activities of employees in combination with other resources to accomplish organisational objectives'. The task of management, this writer goes on, is 'to facilitate the organisation's effectiveness and long-term goal attainment by co-ordinating and efficiently utilising available resources' (Steers, 1991).

However, as numerous writers have pointed out, the term 'manager' covers a vast range of activities and functions from occupying a senior executive position in a huge multinational to running a small branch of a bank or supermarket chain. Accordingly it is usual when discussing this very broad stratum to distinguish within it in terms of *level* and *function*. In relation to level we can distinguish between executives, middle management and first-line management. Executive managers are at the top of the organisation and, if not actually sitting on the board, report directly to a board member. Middle managers are obviously in the middle of the hierarchy and are responsible for the firm's major departments and will oversee the activities of first-line managers. The latter will supervise rank-and-file employees in the day-to-day running of the various departments. The point is that the nature of the activity of managing will vary significantly with level. Generally speaking we can say that the higher up in the hierarchy a manager is, the more likely will he/she be engaged in monitoring business activities and long-range planning. The lower down the hierarchy we move the more likely it is that managers will be concerned with the routine supervision of everyday work tasks. Even so we should not assume that executive managers and middle managers at upper levels spend most of their time at work behind a desk poring over reports, thinking, analysing, reaching decisions after a systematic examination of all the relevant evidence. Countless studies reveal that managers at all levels spend a disproportionate amount of their time *talking* to people. That is, the bulk of the typical manager's day is spent meeting colleagues, superiors and subordinates, discussing, negotiating and trying to sort out problems. Management work, then, is essentially *interactive* rather than contemplative. Contemplative tasks such as report reading and writing have to be fitted in where possible, which often means taken home.

Box 5.3 Key features of managerial work

---

1. Combines a specialist (for example, production, finance, personnel) element with a more general managerial dimension.
2. Much time is spent on dealing with unanticipated problems and disruptions to orderly workflow.
3. Much time is spent in face-to-face verbal encounters of limited duration, asking, persuading, cajoling others to do things. Much managerial work involves coping with social and technical conflict.

4. Little time is spent on any single activity, particularly on the conscious formulation of plans. Planning and decision-making have to be fitted in with other activities.
5. Managers spend a good deal of time explaining and accounting for what they do. This will often involve building up support through informal networks, that is through 'politicking'.
6. Managerial roles carry a good deal of discretion. That is, there is a fair amount of choice as to what is to be done and how. This discretion also runs to deciding where the manager's role begins and ends.

Source: Adapted from C. P. Hales (1986) 'What Managers Do', *Journal of Management Studies*, vol. 23, no. 1, pp. 88–115.

Turning to differences in terms of function, it should be obvious that a manager working in the area of sales spends his/her time dealing with a quite different set of issues and problems from that of his/her colleague working in production, purchasing or personnel. Finance, purchasing, production, sales, personnel and industrial relations is one fairly unexceptionable way of distinguishing the main areas of activity that one would typically encounter in a large manufacturing corporation. It is important to appreciate that these areas or departments differ not only in terms of what they do but also in relation to their perceived centrality to the firm's principal goals. That is to say, certain functions may be seen as more important, as having higher status than others. In Britain, for example, it seems that accounts and finance has a much higher status than it does on the continent. Personnel and its offshoot, corporate affairs, are often seen as fairly peripheral areas, the latter one of the first to be targeted in the event of cutbacks. The main point is that although all the managers in any one enterprise are 'working for the same firm' relationships between departments are often characterised by a good deal of friction and rivalry. That is to say, a considerable amount of the manager's time may be devoted to 'wheeling and dealing' and 'doing down' rivals. For these reasons certain highly respected writers on management have emphasised the centrality of managerial *politics* to an understanding of how organisations actually work.

Modern managers, we have seen, owe their position to a combination of expertise and performance, hence the idea of the 'professional' manager. In relation to the question of expertise it is worth pointing out that the emphasis given to formal qualifications and training varies significantly from country to country. For example 85 per cent of top managers in the United States and Japan have university degrees, 65 per cent in France, 62 per cent in West Germany, but only 27 per cent in Britain. The low figure for Britain seems to reflect what was then (late seventies) the typical British approach to management. This placed greater emphasis on common sense, on-the-job experience and background than on formal training. In relation to background there has been in Britain a pronounced tendency for individuals of middle-class background to be overrepresented in the upper echelons of management. In 1972, for example, nearly 50 per cent of those in Social Class I (higher administrative and managerial) had fathers in the same social category. Only 15 per cent had fathers in the manual sector even though this category represented 51 per cent of the labour force. The higher up the managerial hierarchy one goes the stronger the connection with middle- and upper-middle-class background. This is particularly evident if we look at the proportion of top managers and directors who went to public schools: 80 per cent of directors of clearing banks, 77 per cent of those of merchant banks and 68 per cent of the directors of 40 major industrial firms (figures refer to 1971). Thus the idea that top managers need to be 'the right type' rather than technically qualified seems to be well-entrenched in British culture. By contrast 54 per cent of directors of West Germany's 100 largest companies have doctorates in engineering, science or law!

Since the early seventies, however, business education in Britain has expanded rapidly. This is reflected in the fact that younger managers tend to have received more formal education. But despite this, recent studies show that the majority of managers at all levels in Britain receive little or no formal training other than short-term induction programmes. Most are left to acquire their managerial skills through coping with day-to-day problems at work. The relative absence of formal training goes some way to explaining the low level of mobility amongst British managers. Over half of the managers included in a British Institute of Management survey in the late seventies had been working for their present company for more than ten years. The traditional pattern was for prospective managers to start their careers in technical or routine clerical positions and work their way up through the firm. With the more recent emphasis on formal training, however, this pattern is breaking down with about a third of new entrants moving directly into management as their first job. Direct entry at management level is particularly typical of managers who had previously attended public school. One of the most startling facts to emerge from the BIM survey was the tiny proportion of women managers. Although women constituted 42 per cent of the labour force in the late seventies they accounted for less than 1 per cent of managers. Since then the proportion of women managers has increased quite substantially but still (according to a survey carried out in the late eighties) stands at only 14 per cent. According to the same survey more women managers have university degrees than men (37 per cent as opposed to 22 per cent), a fact that is almost certainly related to women managers tending to be younger than their male counterparts. Women are overrepresented in junior levels of management and in certain areas, notably personnel, training and industrial relations. The survey (comprising 375 managers) found no women managers in production. The same study also found that women managers earned less then men: 20 per cent of men as opposed to 2 per cent of women were earning more than £20 000 per annum. (Data from R. Scase and R. Goffee (1939) *Reluctant Managers*.)

SMALL FIRMS

The drift towards industrial concentration should by no means allow us to overlook the role of the small firm in advanced capitalist economies. Small firms continue to employ a sizeable proportion of the labour force and are especially important in certain areas of the economy. This is particularly the case with services, significantly the most rapidly expanding sector in advanced industrial economies. However, before we turn to consider the long-term future of the small firm we need to decide what we mean by this term.

There have been numerous attempts at delimiting this category. A small-scale employer for some writers has less than 10 workers, for others less than 30. Particularly influential has been a definition adopted by the Bolton Report into small businesses in manufacturing, which fixed upon an upper limit of 200. Bolton, however, added three qualifications: the small firm must have a small share of the market in which it operates, it must be managed by its owner in a personalised fashion and not through a formal organisation, and third, it must not be part of a larger grouping so that the owner–manager is free from outside interference. For other writers the small firm is characterised not by the number of people it employs but by the nature of its organisation. Small firms, following Bolton's second qualification, are characterised by flexibility in the sense that they do not have a rigid division of labour. Small firms, in other words, lack the impersonal bureaucracies of large corporations. But even this restriction covers an unacceptably wide range of business situations. Are we justified in including in the same category a firm with 23 machinists and four office staff on the one hand, and on the other, the local chimney sweep who works from home and whose capital is limited to a van, an industrial vacuum cleaner and a telephone?

A useful approach to the problem of diversity within the small-firm category has been proposed by Scase and Goffee. They distinguish between the *self-employed, small employers, owner–controllers* and *owner–directors*. The self-employed work for themselves, employing no wage labour but often depending heavily on the unpaid services of family members, for example, a spouse answering the telephone and completing VAT returns. Small employers work alongside their employees but in addition undertake the managerial task of running the business. Owner–controllers do not work alongside their employees but are solely responsible for administering and managing their own business. Owner–directors control their enterprise through a managerial hierarchy under which managerial tasks are sub-divided and delegated to executives and other senior personnel. Clearly in the case of this last type we are moving out of the small-firm category.

What role do small firms play in an advanced capitalist economy? Marx believed that as capitalism developed the 'petty bourgeoisie' (that is, small-scale businesses) would eventually disappear. Those economically able to survive in increasingly competitive markets could do so only by expanding the scale of their operations. Those who remained small would eventually be forced out with their owners joining the ranks of the proletariat (proletarianisation).

When the Bolton Report appeared in 1971 it looked as though Marx's prediction was in the process of being borne out, at least so far as manufac-turing was concerned. Whereas small manufacturing establishments consti-tuted 44 per cent of all manufacturing establishments in 1924, by 1968 this figure had fallen to 29 per cent. Two fundamental processes seem to account for the decline of the small firm: industrial concentration and the postwar upsurge in state activity.

As we have seen, all Western economies are characterised by a growing concentration of industrial, commercial and financial resources. Where an industry is dominated by a few large enterprises (oligopoly) the corporate giants largely determine overall volumes of trade and price levels. Under such conditions the trading opportunities for small firms may be very lim-ited. In the seventies small firms were holding their own only in agricul-ture, forestry, fishing, construction, distributive trades and miscellaneous services. Nonetheless, in 1971 they still gave employment to 6 million and produced 20 per cent of Gross National Product.

The effects of concentration on small firms have been augmented by increased state involvement in the economy. By 1969 the public sector in Britain accounted for 25 per cent of the employed population and 27 per cent of gross domestic product. The incursion of the state on this scale is held to affect small firms in the following ways: first, where an industry is nationalised the entry and growth of new firms is prevented; second, the purchasing activities of the state tend to be on a grand scale – whether it is the coal industry buying engineering equipment or the civil service desks and stationery – and therefore favour large well-established contractors;

third, the wide range of regulatory controls enforced by the state – for example, with regard to taxation, pensions, health and safety regulations – tend to produce bigger administrative costs for small firms; and, fourth, the level of taxation on profits is sometimes thought to restrict the ability of small companies.

In addition to these economic constraints, until the seventies the climate of opinion was not favourable to small businesses. Generally speaking they were regarded as inefficient anachronisms unable to take advantage of new technology and sophisticated management systems. Government policy tended to favour large-scale units of production because only they could reap substantial economies of scale. By the end of the seventies, however, this strategy was coming under increasing attack. There was no sign that rationalisation and the promotion of mergers had done much to reduce Britain's perennial problems of poor competitiveness, low productivity, poor quality, low employee motivation and turbulent industrial relations. Accordingly the eighties saw the emergence of a new attitude to the small firm; regarded as something of an economic dinosaur in the sixties it was now to form the core of a revitalised entrepreneurial culture.

But it is not only the ideological climate that seems to favour the small firm. It is important to appreciate that this change in thinking coincides with certain economic and technological developments. First, the growing intensity of competition between large corporations, both at the national and international level, has led many of them to unload some of their operations on to small firms under a variety of subcontracting, franchising or licensing arrangements. In manufacturing and engineering a growing number of large firms 'put out' areas of production to small enterprises. Large retailing chains buy in for resale goods produced by small units. Under such arrangements investment and labour costs are borne by the small firm. It is not unusual for the larger partner to advance loans to small enterprises for the modernisation of plant and premises. However such agreements are often heavily weighted in favour of the lender.

Second, high levels of unemployment and redundancy have forced a growing number to start up on their own using severance payments or savings as initial capital. In principle, business start-up is now made easier by two factors: much of future economic expansion, it is argued, will be in the services sector which in terms of outlay is much less demanding than the generally capital-intensive (but now declining) manufacturing sector. If we look at some of the growth areas in the services sector in the eighties – estate agents, financial services, market research, travel agents, employment agencies, various consultancies – little in the way of start-up capital is needed: rented premises and a telephone.

In addition to the above, the revolution in information technology has facilitated the emergence and survival of small firms in two ways: the availability of accounting, stock control and data storage packages substantially reduces the administrative burden on the small enterprise; and second, developments in such areas as desktop publishing and graphic design and layout have opened up new business opportunities for the individual with small amounts of capital. However, although the current economic and technological climate may seem extremely favourable for the small firm, we must remember that their failure rate, particularly during the early stages, is spectacularly high. Small firms are much less able than large to weather the vicissitudes of normal economic life such as downturns in the market or high interest rates.

CONCLUSION

We have seen in this chapter that as capitalist industrialisation advanced not only did firms increase in size but market economies throughout the world were characterised by a growing concentration of the means of production. Hence advanced capitalism has taken on a distinctly oligopolistic character. The increasing size of the corporation and in many cases the geographical dispersal of its divisions necessitated the growth of formal organisation, namely, hierarchical bureaucracies based upon rational-legal (that is, impersonal) rules and procedures. And to coordinate these bureaucracies, to make them run as smoothly as possible, a stratum of professional managers was needed. Whilst since time immemorial the economic enterprise has always needed to be 'managed' in the most general of senses, the complexities of running the modern corporation are such as to require the knowledge and skills of a group of specialists. Accordingly, this century has seen an explosion of management training, indeed of a management 'science', a field of study devoted to the problem of coordinating the activities of large numbers of people whilst at the same time maintaining high levels of motivation and interest. In fact it is no exaggeration to claim that the task of 'integrating the individual into the organisation' (the title of a well-known book on organisations) has dominated industrial civilisation for most of this century. In the next two chapters we will examine the major contours of this problem.

However, before moving on, we should note once more that the development of oligopolistic capitalism has not led to the disappearance of the small firm. On the contrary, it has been argued that the relentless drive to lower costs is increasingly forcing the corporate giants to contract out more and more of their lines to small firms. In addition the microchip revolution seems set to make conditions more favourable to the survival of small businesses. Indeed it has been argued that the flexibility and speed of communication made possible by microchip technology is leading to a resurgence, even rise to predominance, of the artisan (electronic) workshop. However, this argument we shall return to consider after we have examined some of the principal problems of work organisations.

BIBLIOGRAPHY

Davis, H. and Scase, R. (1985) *Western Capitalism and State Socialism: An Introduction* (Oxford: Blackwell).

Handy, C. *et al*. (1987) *The Making of Managers* (National Economic Development Council).

Kerr, C. *et al*. (1974) *Industrialism and Industrial Man* (Harmondsworth: Penguin).

Lawrence, P. (1984) *Management in Action* (London: Routledge & Kegan Paul).

Mullins, L. J. (1989) *Management and Organisational Behaviour* (London: Pitman).

Pollard, S. (1984) *The Development of the British Economy 1914–1980* (London: Edward Arnold).

Scase, R. and Goffee, R. (1987) *The Real World of the Small Business Owner* (London: Croom Helm).

Scase, R. and Goffee, R. (1989) *Reluctant Managers* (London: Unwin Hyman).

Steers, R. M. (1991) *Introduction to Organisational Behaviour* (London: Harper Collins).

Weber, M. (1964) *The Theory of Social and Economic Organisation* (London: The Free Press).

6 The Organisation of Work

One of the most significant aspects of the Industrial Revolution was that it eventually produced a situation in which the bulk of the working population spent half of their waking lives working in large organisations. We saw in the previous chapter that most adults in Britain, as well as in other advanced capitalist societies, are employed by firms with more than 500 workers. That this figure appears unsensational to us is an indication of the degree to which we are acclimatised to a world dominated by large organisations. However it is worth pondering on the fact that such a situation is a very recent development; that throughout the bulk of human history men and women have lived and worked in small groups, usually the family. Only with the maturing of the Industrial Revolution – in Britain, well into the second half of the nineteenth century – does work in the large firm, the factory, become the norm.

THE PROBLEM OF LABOUR DISCIPLINE

As we saw in the previous chapter, producing on a large scale demands more rigid forms of organisation. Clearly if one is employing hundreds, let alone thousands, of workers it is essential that they all turn up at the requisite time. Since centralised production makes for much closer interdependence between the various sub-processes, it is equally essential that workers in separate departments labour more or less at a constant speed, that they take their breaks according to a strict schedule and that they do not leave before the appointed time. All this may seem painfully obvious to us but it is nonetheless certain that the first recruits to the industrial system did not adapt quickly or easily to the regimentation of factory life. Evidence from pre-industrial societies generally clearly indicates that work was not characterised by the regular intensity – the nine-till-five, five-days-a-week, 48-weeks-a-year pattern that we accept without question. As we now know, work in the pre-industrial period was primarily work on the land. It is not difficult to appreciate that the intensity of agricultural work varies with the seasons, at harvest time occupying virtually all daylight hours, but during certain winter months demanding very little at all. Whilst handicraft industry was not directly affected by the seasons it seems that there also the pace of work varied considerably. During the early days of the week the artisan, his family and their helpers would take it easy even to the extent of doing no work at all on Mondays. The tradition of 'St Monday' when workers took the day off in order to recover from the weekend's carousing persisted well into the industrial period and excited the wrath of many a merchant waiting on finished goods:

> When the framework knitters or makers of silk stockings had a great price for their work, they have been observed seldom to work on Mondays and Tuesdays but to spend most of their time at the ale-house or nine-pins...The weavers, 'tis common with them to be drunk on Monday, have their headache on Tuesday and their tools out of order on Wednesday. (Complaint in 1681 quoted by E. P. Thompson)

Towards the end of the week the pace of work would have to be speeded up considerably for the family to earn enough to meet its basic needs. We need to recall at this point that before the age of mass consumption the acquisitive instincts that we accept as normal were not developed at all. When given a choice most pre-industrial workers preferred more leisure to greater reward. Hence William Hutton, a framework knitter, observed in the 1740s, 'if a man can support his family with three days labour, he will not work six'. This work pattern, characterised by alternate bouts of intense activity and idleness, had been so deeply entrenched over the centuries, indeed millennia, as to become virtually part of human nature. It is not surprising, therefore, that the early industrialists faced a serious problem of labour indiscipline. Nonetheless, the problem was overcome. By the 1850s a majority of British adults probably accepted the factory system and the division of the day into minutes and seconds which it entailed, as a necessary part of human existence. How was this revolution – and it was a 're-volution' – in working habits achieved? This was an extremely complex process but it would be useful at this stage in the discussion to highlight four of the principal contributory factors: economic necessity, the resort to the 'iron fist', mass education and employer paternalism.

Economic necessity

Whilst acquisitive instincts may not have been well-developed before this century, human beings clearly had to acquire the wherewithal to provide themselves with food, clothing and shelter. If, again, we compare the pre-industrial to the industrial period we note a major difference in terms of access to the means of production. Prior to the Industrial Revolution most families had access to land or to simple machinery and very often some combination of both. These means of production could therefore be employed directly to produce food (for consumption or for sale) and/or to manufacture goods for sale. Industrialisation is always associated with the decline of agricultural employment as people leave the countryside for jobs in the towns and cities.

Industrialisation also led to the decline of handicraft industries – spinning, weaving, knitting – as human skills were transferred to machines. The Industrial Revolution thus produced an urban labour force which, no longer having access to its own means of production, necessarily had to sell its labour for a wage. Put simply, whilst he or she (and in the early stages most were women and children) may have detested life in the factories, the first proletarians had to grin and bear it because there was no alternative.

The iron fist

Economic necessity may have got the workers into the factories but it did not guarantee that they would be punctual or exhibit the diligence and commitment which the employers desired. Not only did the labouring class continue to turn up late and display generally dilatory attitudes towards the work, but, even more provoking, many of its members tended to drift away for several days or even weeks once they had earned enough to tide them over. Hence pioneer industrialist, Josiah Wedgwood: 'Our men have been at play four days this week it being Burslem wakes.' Again we note the continuing influence of the pre-industrial era when the calendar was littered with saints' days, holidays, fairs and wakes so that the 'working year' was almost certainly less than one-third of the current 48 weeks. In their drive to break such 'desultory habits of work' the employers introduced a ferociously disciplinarian work regime with drastic punishments such as dismissal for minor infringements of the rules and fines for latecoming and other misdemeanours. In 1821 the rules of one flax mill stated that if an overseer of a room be found talking to a person from another section during working hours he should be dismissed immediately. Everyone in this mill – overseers, mechanics, spinners, reelers – had his/her clearly-laid-down duties, any transgression of which led to instant dismissal. The rules of another mill stated that any person found from their usual work station would be fined 2*d* (two old pence) for the offence. Wedgwood fined his wayward labourers 2/6*d* for throwing things away or leaving fires burning overnight. A fine of 2/6*d* was the penalty for being absent on Monday mornings from the coalmines in Worsley (Lancs.). Mining in fact was one of the most heavily fined occupations with average weekly deductions of 1/--2/- out of a weekly wage of 13/-. Factory gates were closed one minute after the starting siren sounded and the doors of workrooms were often kept locked during working hours. Wedgwood was the first employer, so far as we know, to introduce the time-clock, a device which furnished mechanical proof of lateness and so provided a 'scientific' basis for deductions from wages. The practice soon developed of making the deductions considerably greater than actual time lost. (Fifteen minutes loss of pay for one minute's lateness seems to have become the standard ratio.) 'Clocking in' was to become and continues to be the most potent symbol of factory work. Through these and other methods (not excluding the physical abuse of women and children) the factory owners, or rather their deputies, initiated the new industrial army into the drills and routines of the factory system.

Mass education

During the first half of the nineteenth century formal education for the masses was, to say the least, haphazard in England, confined largely to private 'dame' schools or to that provided voluntarily by the churches and employers. For most children it was virtually non-existent. Thus by 1851 out of nearly five million children of school age 600 000 were at work and two million in school. The remainder was in neither. Consequently as we enter the second half of the century the churches and middle-class reformers are becoming increasingly concerned not only about the extent of illiteracy, but that such large numbers of children should pass their days roaming the streets apparently unrestrained by any form of external discipline. It should be made clear that there was a firm belief amongst the ruling classes that there was a direct connection between ignorance and social disorder. As a mid-century church inquiry warned, 'discontent and insubordination were most rife in quarters which least enjoyed the advantages of education'. Accordingly as education was extended to the masses under the dual authority of church and state it is not surprising that a heavy emphasis was placed on discipline. Far from fostering critical faculties or raising awareness mass education was confined to the strictly useful three Rs and the performance of simple mechanical tasks. This was backed up by a concerted drive to inculcate habits of obedience, punctuality, personal cleanliness and respect for authority. Given the dominant influence of the church at this time it is to be expected that religion – hymn-singing, homilies emphasising the connection between 'good' behaviour and just deserts – formed a significant part of the programme. The key point is that not only did this type of education aim to transform little boys and girls into respectable 'citizens', it also prepared them for the monotonous routine of the world of work.

Employer paternalism

Mass education was not, of course, completely successful in changing disorderly proletarians into passive obedient servants. Far from it: protest against the conditions and deprivations imposed by the industrial system continued to erupt. But the more we move into the second half of the century the more frequently this protest takes an organised form. That is to say the working class increasingly articulates its needs and interests through the medium of the trade union. This is to be contrasted with the more anarchic forms of protest such as machine-breaking – 'collective bargaining by riot' as one historian, Eric Hobslaum, has termed it – that typified the early 1800s. At mid-century, trade union membership probably stood at less than 250 000 whereas by 1888 it had tripled to three-quarters of a million. (However this was still only 5 per cent of the labour force as a whole, 10 per cent of the male labour force.) It seems certain that the growth of trade unions and the increasing confidence it expressed was a key factor in persuading more enlightened industrialists of the need to win the *consent* of their employees rather than relying solely on repression. Accordingly a distinctly paternalistic strain becomes much more apparent in the second half of the century. Innovations such as works dinners, canteens, libraries, gymnasia, burial societies and annual trips to the seaside become increasingly available as 'fringe benefits' for the employees of large enterprises. Some employers provided their workers with schools and housing and even built model towns for them. In the 1850s Sir Titus Salt moved his alpaca and mohair mills out of Bradford to the specially created new town of Saltaire, an employer's town supposedly benevolently administered. In 1879 work commenced on the building of George Cadbury's Bournville and in 1888 Port Sunlight was begun by soap magnate W. H. Lever. The administration of Port Sunlight was to be an extension of the firm's new-found interest in 'labour – management' relations.

It should be made clear that these and other less ambitious examples do not mean that after 1850 British industrialists underwent a mass conversion to paternalism and other forms of 'do-goodery'. The philanthropic thrust did not replace but intermingled with the earlier *laissez-faire* (that is, profits-at-all-costs) impulse. Paternalism was, after all, a more sophisticated form of self-interest and the fringe benefits, anyway, were usually paid for either directly or indirectly, by the labour force itself. Nonetheless, the paternalistic upsurge represented among the employing classes a growing understanding that coercion was not enough to make the modern enterprise truly efficient.

THE EVASION OF MANAGEMENT

Despite these steps in the direction of some conception of 'management', management in the sense of the systematic application of a 'science' of workplace relations is a late arrival on the European industrial scene. Not until after the First World War do we observe on anything like a significant scale the practical employment of management theory. Throughout the nineteenth century management in most industries was evaded in the sense that the main tasks of supervision and administration were hived off to various non-managerial institutions. The three most important of these were the family, the subcontracting system and the foreman.

In the early stages of the Industrial Revolution a number of continuities with the pre-industrial era are readily observable. One of the most apparent was the family which, having previously furnished the basis of production, retained many aspects of this function within the factory system. If we look at spinning, the core industry of the transformation in Britain, it was the custom until the 1820s for the skilled cotton spinner to provide his own assistants. Under the circumstances it was logical to 'employ' his wife and children not least because he already exerted authority over them. The factory-owner paid only the head of the family who then supports them in whatever way is deemed appropriate. However from the 1820s on, technological advances in spinning, weaving and elsewhere made necessary a larger number of assistants, larger than family ties could produce. It is in this situation that we can observe a transition from family-based production to subcontracted teams. Under this system the subcontractor negotiates with the owner a price for a particular volume of work. It is then up to the subcontractor to provide labour, tools and in some cases raw materials, and to supervise operations. Such arrangements have a number of advantages for the owner: the tasks of supervising, coordinating and disciplining labour are delegated to the contractor, who, since his return depends upon how much profit he can make out of the deal, has a direct interest in getting his team to work with maximum efficiency. Administrative overheads are reduced since the contractor works out wages and systems of payment. Technical problems with which the owner may be ill-equipped to deal can be left for the contractor to sort out. And last, subcontracting is particularly suited to a fluctuating market: where the owner has no personal links with individual members of the contract team – they are not his employees – lay-offs can be achieved with a minimum of fuss.

Subcontracting obviously survives today and with the recent quest by employers for a more flexible labour force is almost certainly coming back into favour. However, from a nineteenth-century perspective subcontracting as a general system began to decline in the 1880s and 1890s. This was the era of the so-called 'Great Depression' when falling prices seriously squeezed profits and in the process the subcontractor tended to fall by the wayside. The situation was in fact extremely complicated, but for our purposes we can say that as firms grew in size and as the labour force stabilised, employers found it cheaper and more convenient to delegate the main tasks of management to their principal supervisory employee – the foreman. Before the First World War the foreman's role embraced a wide range of functions: as well as supervising production, he acted as planner, cost clerk, administrator and personnel officer. It was normal for example, for foremen to enjoy the authority to hire and fire. The state of the labour market and low levels of unionisation endowed him with considerable power and this was frequently used in an arbitrary fashion – to reward friends by giving them easy jobs as well as to make life difficult for any employee who challenged his authority. The decline of the foreman from being the principal agent of management to merely a first-line supervisor is inextricably bound up with the development of the large firm. The accompanying bureaucratisation of the enterprise meant that what had been the foreman's functions were successively taken over by departments: recruitment and training by personnel; supervision by production and quality control; product improvement by research and development; payments by accounts and finance and so on. The increasing complexity of technology, of the division of labour, of production, purchasing, marketing and of systems of payment as well as, with the expansion of the power and influence of the trade unions, of labour relations – such complexity made it more and more difficult for the factory owners to continue with management on an individual piecemeal basis. Large size, in other words, made the centralisation and standardisation of management inevitable. The various management functions had to be condensed into a series of standard rules and procedures, all of which meant that management had to be conceived as a systematic activity.

Given the link between size and management thinking it is not surprising that, since the large corporation first emerged there, the United States took the lead in this field. In fact the mere mention of management as a science immediately conjures up the figure of F. W. Taylor. Although Taylor was by no means the first to think about the problems of management and their likely solutions, he was undoubtedly industrial society's first global apostle of the new creed of scientific management.

TAYLORISM

Frederick Winslow Taylor (1856–1917) trained as an engineer before joining Midvale Steelworks initially as a labourer but working his way up to the position of chief engineer. Taylor subsequently became a management consultant and devoted prodigious energy to promoting his ideas about management. He first published his views on management in a paper, 'A Piece-rate System', which was read to the American Society of Engineers in 1895. This paper was expanded into a book, *Shop Management* (1905). But by far his best-known work is *Principles of Scientific Management*, published in 1911. For Taylor the primary object of management is to maximise the prosperity of both employers and employees. Maximum prosperity means not simply the largest possible short-term gain for both parties, but the development of all aspects of the enterprise in the interests of efficiency. Such prosperity is within easy reach if only management and labour would grasp what for Taylor was abundantly self-evident: their mutual interdependence and the need for them to work together. Not only did neither party seldom recognise this basic fact of life, but the normal state of relations between them was characterised by antagonism and mistrust. Why? Taylor suggests three principle reasons: first, the erroneous belief among workers that increases in output will inevitably lead to unemployment; second, defective systems of management which make it necessary for each worker to restrict his output in order to protect his interests (what Taylor termed 'systematic soldiering'); and third, inefficient rule-of-thumb methods of work which result in much wasted effort. The aim of *scientific* management is to overcome these obstacles, first, through the systematic study of the work process, the aim being to discover the most efficient way of performing each and every work task, and second, through the systematic study of management in order to determine the most effective methods of controlling and directing the labour force.

The basic character of Taylor's approach can be brought out with a much-quoted example taken from his time as a management consultant at Bethlehem Steel. The problem Taylor confronted was how to increase the productivity of a group of men engaged in loading pig-iron. Taylor selected a Dutch labourer, Schmidt, whom Taylor identified as a 'high-priced man', that is, someone who placed a high value on earning as much as possible. After prolonged observation of the task in hand Taylor gave Schmidt detailed instructions on the number of paces to walk, when to sit and rest and so on. As a consequence Schmidt attained an output of 47 tons a day when the shift average had previously been 12 tons. When the other labourers in the group were trained in the same methods only one in eight could achieve Schmidt's rate. Nonetheless each one of them increased his productivity. This example enables us to bring out the essentials of Taylor's system:

(a) The need for the scientific selection and training of workers;
(b) The need for the scientific observation of the task in hand. Taylor believed that there is always one best way of doing a particular job and that using the 'time study' – carefully timing each component movement – was the best way to find it.
(c) The need for the appropriate organisational back-up for each and every work task to be performed within a given plant. Identifying the best way of doing a job always has implications for the organisation at large. In the above example the supply and storage of tools, the delivery times and removal of the pig-iron – all have a bearing on the actual task of loading. It is essential that the daily duties of every workman be planned in advance and that each receive written instructions detailing what is to be done and how with the time allowed;
(d) The need for a proper incentive scheme which would derive maximum productivity and in the process permit each worker to earn as much as possible.

Taylor firmly believed that the proper application of his 'science' would convince the labour force that striving for the highest productivity possible was in their own interests. Scientific management would therefore eliminate industrial conflict for it would demonstrate to both sides of industry that their interests were fundamentally identical. Trade unions would therefore become redundant. In fact Taylor was hostile to trade unions because he believed that the collective agreements they negotiated in setting a standard rate for the job penalised those individuals who wanted to work harder and earn more. Taylor's ideal situation would be one in which there is a different rate of pay for each worker according to his/her alleged ability.

Despite these optimistic claims the implementation of Taylor's ideas at Bethlehem Steel provoked such resentment among the labour force that management asked him to dilute his methods. Unwilling to compromise Taylor left Bethlehem and moved to the Watertown Arsenal where he began his time studies in June 1911. But again scientific management excited the hostility of the workforce to such a degree as to unleash a strike.

This event and the general notoriety Taylor's ideas were acquiring attracted the attention of the United States Government which deputed its Commission on Industrial Relations to look into them. The Commission, before which Taylor himself testified, concluded that whilst his science contained many useful techniques and offered some valuable suggestions, its implementation shifted the balance of power too far in the direction of management. Official misgivings about Taylorism led to the time study method being banned in all government establishments.

Taylor accepted that the introduction of his methods had indeed aroused hostility and caused strikes. But this, he maintained, was because they had been introduced too quickly with inadequate preparation. Considerable effort must be directed to securing the cooperation of the workforce and persuading its members that reducing work tasks to their simplest elements was not against their interests. On the contrary, by allowing significant increases in production and hence profits, this would enable workers to earn more. It is therefore to the worker's advantage to adapt to the standardised system management has devised for him/her. The employee who cannot accept that the new system will work in his own interests either does not understand it properly or it has been misrepresented by workmates or trade unionists.

Box 6.1 The spread of Taylorism

Taylor's methods were soon adopted by many firms in the United States, Britain and Europe. After Taylor died in 1915 his ideas were developed by other enthusiasts of 'scientific' management. One of Taylor's most prominent followers in the United States, Frank Gilbreth, added the study of motion to the time study. The 'time and motion' study aims to break down work tasks into a series of elementary bodily movements known as 'therbligs' (Gilbreth's name spelt 'backwards'). In addition to the stopwatch the time and motion study employed the chronocyclograph – a photograph of the workplace on which 'motion paths' could be superimposed. Subsequently movie cameras were incorporated into the scientific study of physical movements. In one form or another the time and motion study – embodied in the time and motion inspector with his stopwatch – has become as central a symbol of modern industry as clocking in.

Another well-known Taylorite, Charles E. Bedaux, was born in Paris in 1886 but emigrated to the United States at the age of 20. After doing an assortment of jobs, mostly in the field of sales, Bedaux went to work for a furniture company in Michigan. There he developed the system that was to make his fortune.

The Bedaux system is shrouded in pseudo-scientific language but at its heart is a basic unit of labour measurement known as the 'B'. The 'B' is a 60-second work unit which also includes a brief period for rest. The appeal of the system was that it promised to make possible the systematic comparison of work tasks in different situations, across departments and even factories. It thus seemed to offer to managers a monitoring and control system which provided a total picture of all work activity in a given plant. Although Bedaux, like Taylorites generally, greatly overestimated the potential 'rationality' of organisational structures and techniques his system acquired considerable popularity in the world of emerging corporations. In 1937 it was being operated in 500 firms in the United States, 225 in Britain and 145 in France. By then Bedaux had made enough money to retire to a château in France where he spent his days entertaining prominent Nazis along with the Duke and Duchess of Windsor.

On Bedaux see Craig Littler (1986) *The Development of the Labour Process in Capitalist Societies*, ch. 8.

Despite apprehension on the part of some, Taylor's ideas spread rapidly in the United States, Britain and on the Continent. Even in Russia after the Bolshevik Revolution of 1917 they were enthusiastically embraced by Soviet head of state, V. I. Lenin, who saw scientific management as part of the solution to the problem of his country's economic backwardness. There is no doubt that Taylorism in its various forms (see Box 6.1) made possible prodigious increases in production. It is, furthermore, no exaggeration to state that the major elements of Taylor's system – identifying and separating out the components of work tasks, the systematic scheduling of sequences of tasks throughout the plant, inspection between operations, standardisation of methods and equipment, more systematic and continuous use of equipment, inventory controls – all came to form the core of modern management. For our purposes the most salient feature, and for many writers the heart, of Taylorism is its radical separation of mental from manual labour. Under Taylorism a knowledgeable management *plans* whilst a knowledgeless workforce *does*. For this reason Taylorism is heavily criticised over the extent to which it removes skills from jobs and is charged with reducing men and women to the status of machines. The breaking-up of production into a series of simple tasks (job fragmentation) is held to deprive work of meaning and a sense of fulfilment. Taylorism, some go so far as to claim, has significantly contributed to the alienation of the worker from both his/her product and society.

These criticisms we shall return to as they are at the centre of all discussions of work in modern society. Let us first look at another series of studies again carried out in the United States but more than a decade after Taylor. Like Taylorism the Hawthorne studies launched a major reorientation in thinking about the modern enterprise and those who spend half their waking lives working in it.

ELTON MAYO AND HAWTHORNE

Elton Mayo (1880–1949) was to become a pioneer in the then developing field of industrial psychology. His first major study in the early 1920s was concerned with the problem of very high labour turnover in the spinning department of a Pennsylvania textile mill. In the study Mayo attempted to explore the relationships between different types of rest period and productivity. Between 1927 and 1932, now at the Harvard Business School, Mayo supervised a major research project at Western Electric's Hawthorne works in Chicago. Western Electric was preoccupied with the problem of productivity and before Mayo and his team came into the plant had carried out its own investigation into the effects of illumination on output. The firm's experimenters assumed that as illumination improved so productivity would increase, which indeed it did. The problem was that when using an experimental group of workers output continued to increase even when there was a marked decrease in illumination. How then was one to explain the rise in production?

With this kind of question in mind Mayo began his first series of experiments in the Relay Assembly Room where women were engaged in assembling electrical switches. Initially the weekly production of six of the women was recorded in their normal work situation. The six were then moved to a special test room where they could be observed by a research worker. There followed a number of periods during which certain changes were introduced into this experimental work situation – a new system of remuneration, rest pauses varied in length, snacks provided during breaks, the length of the working day varied – and their effects recorded. The outstanding result of this 26-month experiment was an almost uninterrupted rise in average hourly and total weekly production. This was despite the fact that conditions were exactly similar in certain periods, and that in one the working day had been substantially lengthened.

Mayo's team attempted to establish a statistical relationship between productivity and a range of factors, for example, changes in work methods and materials, fatigue, monotony, room temperature, hours of sleep and fluctuations in the weather; but without success. Because of these negative findings the experimenters began to shift their attention away from psycho-physical aspects of work towards social factors. The only constant factors throughout the test room experiments were the existence of a small social group, the relatively high stability of its membership, the feelings of mutual loyalty the women developed towards each other, and the special treatment of the group by management – the fact that they had been selected in the first place, plus their being consulted at every stage of the experiment.

In order to explore further the social dimension the team moved on to conduct the Bank Wiring Room study. In this case a team of fourteen men engaged in soldering electricity cables to banks of contacts were closely observed. It was found that the men did not fully understand the incentive scheme that applied to them and that they had developed their own standard of a day's work which was in fact well below what they were actually capable of. Most of them reported this standard output each day whether they had exceeded it or not. A belief was expressed within the group that for unspecified reasons to exceed this norm would be dangerous. Supervisors did not try to break up such practices primarily because they were heavily dependent on the goodwill of the men. They were also compromised by their failure to report non-compliance with the rules. Although there was an overall consensus on output the fourteen tended to divide into three subgroups: the first conformed closest to the agreed norm, a second produced above it, a third below it. The over-producers were known as 'ratebusters' and the under-producers as 'chiselers'. The deviants were criticised in hostile terms, excluded from in-group conviviality and subjected to 'binging' – painful blows on the arm. This study indicated that where relationships with management are not entirely satisfactory primary groups within the labour force will act to restrict output in accordance with elaborate systems of rules and sanctions.

The Relay Assembly and Bank Wiring experiments broke new ground in providing strong support for the hypothesis that primary group identification within the workforce, as well as primary group relations with representatives of management, are crucial variables in the determination of rate of work. This is not to suggest that industrial researchers had been entirely ignorant of the existence of primary groups before, simply that the Hawthorne studies brought out their real significance. The new-found emphasis on the group contrasted not only with the person-centred approach of the industrial psychologist, but particularly with the management (Taylorite) assumption that workers were primarily *individuals* who just happened to be working next to each other.

It is important to appreciate that alongside the two main pieces of research in the test room and the Bank Wiring room Mayo and his team conducted more than 20 000 interviews. During these respondents were asked mainly about their attitudes to their job. As a result comprehensive information was acquired not just about the company and management–worker relations, but concerning matters outside work such as family life and social relationships generally. The experimenters were impressed by the extent to which the interviewees appeared to welcome the opportunity to talk about their feelings and problems and generally 'let off steam' in a relaxed and friendly atmosphere. The interview programme highlighted the importance of management taking account of the human and social aspects of work organisations. In doing so it and the Hawthorne research generally undoubtedly gave a powerful impetus to modern personnel management with its emphasis on counselling and the need to be aware of employees' needs and interests.

The main implication for management of Hawthorne's discovery of the importance of informal groups in the workplace is that they could be used to promote organisational goals. New employees could be linked in with established groups; individuals could be guided away from groups hostile or indifferent to management policy; above all management should identify informal group leaders and use them as communications channels and as a means of bringing the workforce into decision-making and disciplinary procedures. Hawthorne has, in fact, been accused of producing a sociology for managers. The researchers, critics claim, limited their observations to those variables which the manager can manipulate – communication, information and induction procedures – and neglected other institutional and structural variables which could have greater explanatory power, for example, the effects of home and neighbourhood. Mayo and his team are charged with failing to recognise the extent to which the firm is an arena for struggle between diverse and often conflicting groups. Labour organisations, for example, are accorded a very peripheral role both in worker–management relations and as a focus of loyalty and attachment. Sociologist Daniel Bell has gone so far as to label Hawthorne and the Human Relations school which it spawned (Box 6.2) as 'cow sociology', the central aim of which is to create workers who feel contented and satisfied and will therefore produce more.

Whether or not this is the case is less important than the fact that the Human Relations approach embodies a recognition that the psychological needs and social relations in and outside the workplace have a major bearing on output. This contrasts very markedly with Taylor's position which sees the worker only as an individual concerned overwhelmingly with the monetary rewards of work. Taylor was certainly aware of the existence of cliques and friendship groups in the workplace but saw them as important only in so far as they impeded organisational efficiency. The properly run firm would not only eliminate primary groups but, more important, the need for such forms of involvement.

Both Taylor and Mayo believed that the adoption of their respective approaches by management would substantially reduce workplace conflict: Taylor because scientific management would provide the workforce with the organisational means to earn the maximum with a minimum of effort;

Mayo because employee needs and the informal mechanisms set up to meet them could be harmonised with organisational goals. For Taylor the proper task of management is to organise human beings as efficiently as possible; for Mayo it is to humanise the organisation as much as possible.

Box 6.2   The Hawthorne studies and the Human Relations movement

The Hawthorne studies are generally held to have produced the Human Relations movement. However, to talk of a Human Relations 'movement' as though it embodied a clearly defined and distinct perspective would be simplistic. All we can say is that in a very general sense a Human Relations approach assumes the existence of certain human needs, particularly a need for social involvement, and believes that such needs can and should be catered for in the workplace. Elton Mayo himself was very much influenced by the idea that informal workgroups could become the source of identity and focus of belonging that during the pre-industrial era were provided by the village community. Workgroups thus compensate for the absence of community involvement afforded by modern city living. The principal task of the Human Relations-oriented manager is to recognise the existence and significance of informal groups and to strive to harness the energy and expertise within them to the goals of the firm.

However, the problem with many examples of informal behaviour is that they aim precisely to *circumvent* management policy as manifested in formal rules and procedures. For this reason the activities in which informal workgroups engage have been termed 'strategies of independence'. The output restrictions of Hawthorne's bank wirers are an obvious example. A good deal of interest has been expressed by industrial sociologists in how employees 'make out' at work, that is to say, how they attain the required daily quota of work with a minimum degree of boredom and fatigue. Working flat out for a period in order to build up a reserve which then allows time for relaxation is one well-known strategy which helps employees to make out. Doubling up – doing some else's job for twenty minutes so that he/she can spend time in the washroom reading the newspaper – is another. Industrial sociologist Donald Roy spent nearly a year working as a radial drill operator in a North American steel plant where he was able to observe closely the stratagems employed by his fellow operatives in their attempts to make out. Many of these focused on the relationship between the operatives and the rate-fixers who used time and motion techniques to determine piece-rates for each job. During the initial run of the job the operative, by resorting to a range of subterfuges, would attempt to convince the rate-fixer that more time was needed to complete it than in reality was necessary. The aim was to obtain a favourable rate, thereby enabling the operative to make out with relative ease. However, the rate-fixer, specially trained and with years of experience behind him, would invariably see through the pretence. (D. Roy (1969) 'Making out: a counter-system of workers' control of work situation and relationships', in T. Burns (ed.), *Industrial Man.*

TECHNOLOGY AND WORK

As already suggested the Hawthorne studies have come under a number of criticisms most of which need not concern us here. However, one theme which may usefully be introduced at this point is the link between technology and the pattern of workplace social interaction. One area not adequately investigated during the Hawthorne research was the extent to which social relations at work are constrained by the organisation of technology. In fact it was not until after the Second World War that this dimension began to be explored systematically. A major advance here was made at the London-based Tavistock Institute of Human Relations during the immediate postwar years. In a paper published in 1951, 'Some Social and Psychological Consequences of the Longwall Method of Coal-getting', E. Trist and K. W. Bamforth examined the impact of mechanisation in the British mining industry. The introduction during the forties of mechanical coal-cutters and conveyor belts made possible the working of a long coalface as opposed to a series of short ones. However, expected gains in productivity did not materialise. On the contrary, where the longwall method was introduced management – worker relations suffered a marked deterioration and absenteeism and accident rates increased.

In their investigation of these problems Trist and Bamforth (the latter an ex-miner) conducted a detailed study of the pattern of social relationships associated with both the traditional shortwall method and the mechanised system which replaced it. The pattern of organisation in the former was based upon a workgroup consisting of a skilled (artisan) miner, his assistant and one or more labourers. The group was self-selected (that is, not predetermined by formal organisation), negotiated its own price for cutting a given area of coalface directly with management, and enjoyed considerable autonomy with regards to methods and pace of working. In addition the workgroup had strong social ties with each other outside work and its members would usually undertake some responsibility for the support of each other's families in the event of injury of death.

The longwall method, by contrast, was organised on a three-shift basis, each shift consisting of 40–50 men employed on one of three basic operations: one shift cut the coal, the second loaded it onto the conveyor belt, whilst the third propped up the roof and moved the machinery into place for the next phase of coal-cutting. This new system obviously destroyed the small workgroups that had been at the heart of its predecessor. Informal cliques did develop but these did not necessarily include every member of each shift. Hostility between shifts developed with each blaming the other for hold-ups and disruptions. Generally speaking, loss of autonomy and group solidarity produced a culture of backbiting, deception, defensiveness and low morale.

Whilst Trist and Bamforth fully understood that there was no going back to the old system they nonetheless believed that there was room for manoeuvre within the new. Accordingly they proposed a third form of operation known as the 'composite longwall method'. This attempted to benefit from the new technology whilst at the same time retaining some of the advantages of the old system. Under the composite system groups of miners were to be responsible for the whole task, allocating themselves to shifts and to jobs within each shift. Bonuses were paid on a group basis. Where operated the composite system overcame the problem of shift specialisation and the scapegoating tendency that this had produced. It was generally claimed that the composite longwall method reaped the technological advantages of mechanisation whilst avoiding the shortcomings of the rigid three-shift system. Productivity increased, absenteeism and accident rates declined and overall job satisfaction improved.

More or less at the same time as Trist and Bamforth were researching the British mining industry, across the Atlantic C. R. Walker and R. H. Guest were interviewing 180 car assemblers about their working lives. The results were published in a book, *Man on the Assembly Line* (1952), which, like Trist and Bamforth's work, has become something of a classic in industrial sociology.

The key features of assembly-line work are that the pace of work is dictated by the speed of the line and is therefore outside the control of the operative. Work tasks are furthermore reduced to the simplest of operations (job fragmentation). Overall the job is repetitive, unskilled, unchallenging and monotonous. Not surprisingly it is thoroughly disliked by the assemblers but not just because of these latter features. A majority of the sample complained that because of the noise and the layout of the line they experienced little social interaction at work. Few respondents were conscious of belonging to any identifiable workgroup and some were cut off from social contacts altogether. Walker and Guest believed that this lack of social contact represented a serious form of deprivation significantly augmenting the negative effects of machine-paced and repetitive work. It was also, they maintained, a key factor behind the high rates of absenteeism and labour turnover that are associated with this type of work. The authors called for more research to explore how far jobs can be redesigned in order to permit more social contacts. They also recommended job enlargement and job rotation to counter the monotony of working on the assembly line.

CONCLUSION

The emergence of large work organisations raised the fundamental problem of acclimatising the industrial labour force to the unrelenting rhythms
of factory life. Whilst market forces – the need to earn a living – forced the
proletariat into the factories, they could not guarantee requisite levels of
output and attention to quality. By resorting to the 'iron fist' – stringent discipline, fines and instant dismissal for minor misdemeanours – employers
hoped to drill the new industrial army into submission. However, the closer
we move to the twentieth century the greater the recognition that coercion
needed to be interlarded with some form of persuasion whether in the form
of monetary incentives or fringe benefits. The appeal of Taylorism, when it
developed in the United States, was that, in linking output solely to monetary incentives, it seemed to eliminate the need for the big stick. So long
as managers could convince their employees that they had so arranged the
work situation as to make it possible for them to earn as much as they
desired, then the problem of integration disappeared. However, Taylorism
suffered from the basic defect that it was based upon an overly simplistic
model of human behaviour. Taylor's conception of Economic Man
assumed that human beings are driven overwhelmingly by their material
interests. The Hawthorne studies revealed that employees do not always
strive to earn as much as they might, often subordinating material to other
needs. Under Hawthorne, Social Man is substituted for Economic Man.

But despite these findings subsequent developments throughout the
industrialised world seemed to have followed Taylorite lines. Planning has
been separated from doing and the work tasks of the 'doers' seem to have
been progressively fragmented or deskilled. This is the dilemma highlighted in the work of Trist and Bamforth and Walker and Guest: that the
drive for ever greater efficiency and higher profits must inevitably transform work into meaningless drudgery. Individual autonomy is reduced to a
minimum, whilst the pace and character of work is more and more dictated
by the machine. And yet both pieces of research suggest that technology is
not wholly determinate, that it is possible to modify working arrangements
within its confines. Thus Trist and Bamforth propose their composite longwall system whilst Walker and Guest advocate job enlargement and rotation. How far these and other proposals represent solutions to meaningless
work we will explore further in the next chapter. First of all, however, we
need to identify more clearly the factors which create the alleged problem
before moving on to examine its extent. This should enable us to decide whether job fragmentation is a general process in advanced industrial
societies or whether it is restricted to certain mainly manual occupations.

BIBLIOGRAPHY

Burns, T. (ed.) (1969) *Industrial Man* (Harmondsworth: Penguin).

Harrison, J. F. C. (1984) *The Common People* (London: Fontana).

Littler, C. (1986) *The Development of the Labour Process in Capitalist Societies* (Aldershot: Gower).

Pugh, D. S. (ed.) (1990) *Organisation Theory* (Harmondsworth: Penguin).

Pugh, D. S. and Hickson, D. J. (1989) *Writers on Organisations* (Harmondsworth: Penguin).

Rose, M. (1988) *Industrial Behaviour* (Harmondsworth: Penguin).

Sofer, C. (1976) *Organisations in Theory and Practice* (London: Heinemann).

Taylor, F. W. (1911) *The Principles of Scientific Management* (New York: Harper & Row).

Thompson, E. P. (1976) 'Time, Work-discipline and Industrial Capitalism', *Past and Present*, vol. 38.

Trist, E. A. and Bamforth, K. W. (1990) 'Some Social and Psychological Consequences of the Longwall Method of Coal-getting' in D. S. Pugh (ed.) *Organisation Theory* (Harmondsworth: Penguin).

Walker, C. R. and Guest, R. H. (1952) *The Man on the Assembly Line* (Cambridge, Mass.: Harvard University Press).

7 Mass Production in Crisis

One of the most significant findings of the research carried out by Walker and Guest (discussed at the end of the previous chapter) was that three-quarters of their sample were prepared to endure the tedium of the assembly line because of the relatively high wages this work paid (for many 5 per cent higher than their previous job). This combination of high pay for unskilled (fragmented) and monotonous work, for many writers, typifies working life in mature industrial societies. The expression 'Fordism' is used to denote not just the character of work but in addition the social and political conditions which form the background to it. The expression derives from the world-famous mass-produced automobile and its inventor, Henry Ford.

HENRY FORD AND FORDISM

In 1903 when the Ford Motor Company was founded the building of auto-mobiles was a highly skilled operation undertaken by craftsmen, all-round mechanics who assembled a complete car on the spot. Five years later this situation had changed only slightly with the emergence of a degree of specialisation between the mechanics, and the addition of teams of 'stockrun-ners' who brought tools and parts to the craftsmen. However, demand for the Model T after it first appeared in 1910 was so great that Ford's engin-eers were under constant and intense pressure to find ways of speeding up production. Eventually the idea of moving car assemblies on a conveyor belt past a fixed number of working stations was developed. This culmin-ated in the inauguration of the first assembly line proper at Ford's Highland Park plant in 1914. Under this system a complete vehicle is assembled from start to finish by adding parts piecemeal as it moves along the line. By 1925 more Model Ts could be produced in a single day than had been pro-duced in a year when the car was first launched. At the same time the price at which the car could be sold fell from $850 to $360 between 1908 and 1916 alone. In order to reduce costs further Ford moved rapidly to uniform rates of pay for all operatives. Since this replaced a complex system of bonuses and incentive schemes the savings in administrative overheads were considerable. This process under which craftsmanship gave way to machine-paced repetitive simple operations with uniform wage rates soon spread to other industries.

But just as the first industrial proletariat did not take easily to the early factory system so, more than a century later, their descendants rejected the assembly line. The most visible indication of this was colossal rates of labour turnover. Ford himself admitted to a labour turnover of 380 per cent in 1914 alone. Not only this, support for unionisation was gathering pace amongst America's working class. Ford's response to the problem of labour turnover and the threat of unionisation was characteristically audacious: at a stroke he raised the basic wage rate from $2.34 to $5 per day. After six months' probation during which his behaviour and morals both inside and outside the plant would be investigated by the company's 'sociology' department, the Ford operative could hope to be on to the 'five-dollar day'. In his autobiography Ford described the five-dollar day as 'one of the finest cost-cutting moves we ever made'. This relatively high rate gave Ford a large pool of labour to draw on. It also cleared the way for the increased regimentation of work because employees were now anxious to hold on to their jobs. Paying higher than average wages locked Ford employees into a particular consumption pattern which made it difficult for them to give up their work, unrewarding though it may have been. This relationship between tedious work, high wages and high levels of consumption, a relationship first signposted by Ford in 1914, was to become, for many writers, one of the fundamental characteristics of capitalism for most of this century.

The point is that Fordist-type mass production made it possible to increase dramatically the amounts produced, thereby permitting substantial cuts in the cost of the items produced. This in turn permitted high wages without eating seriously into profits. These wages could then be spent on mass-produced items assisted by the provision of credit. Prior to the Fordist era (the equivalent of Rostow's age of high mass consumption; see Box 4.2) there had only been a small middle-class market for consumption items such as furniture, clothes, cars, fridges, radios and suchlike. Fordist methods of production made possible the emergence of *mass* markets.

Fordism, however, has two major weak points. The first relates to its economic context, particularly the matching of production to consumption. Clearly, what is produced must be consumed otherwise there will be a crisis of over-production leading to falling prices, recession and possibly slump. The way in which production and consumption were balanced in postwar Europe was through Keynesian policies of intervention, mainly the maintenance of full employment. (In the United States massive defence spending was more important than welfarism in sustaining the level of demand.) But as we saw in Chapter 3, the world recession of the seventies led to the abandonment of Keynesianism and the adoption of monetarism.

However, the broader socioeconomic consequences for Fordism and its decline we must leave to the final chapter.

Let us first look at the impact of mass-production techniques on the actual work experience itself. As already suggested, the pioneering work of Walker and Guest clearly demonstrated the negative side of assembly-line work in terms of high levels of worker discontent. Their findings have been corroborated by numerous other studies, including Robert Blauner's much-quoted *Alienation and Freedom* (1964). Central to Blauner's research is the notion of alienation, a concept which has acquired considerable significance in German philosophy and which plays a central role in Marx's early writings.

WORK AND ALIENATION

Although he was by no means the first to apply the term 'alienation', to the human condition, it is Marx's usage that has been most influential in sociology. Below is an extract from Marx's *Paris Manuscripts* (1844) in which he outlines the four levels of alienation: alienation from the product of one's labour, from the process of production and productive activity generally, from one's fellow human beings and from one's essential nature:

> The worker is related to the product of his labour as to an alien object. The object he produces does not belong to him, dominates him, and only serves in the long run to increase his poverty. Alienation appears not only in the result, but also in the process of production and productive activity itself. The worker is not at home in his work which he views only as a means of satisfying other needs. It is an activity directed against himself, that is independent of him and does not belong to him. Thirdly, alienated labour succeeds in alienating man from his species. Species life, productive life, life creating life, turns into a mere means of sustaining the worker's individual existence, and man is alienated from his fellow men. Finally, nature itself is alienated from man, who thus loses his own inorganic body. (Quoted in David McLellan (1971) *The Thought of Karl Marx*, p. 107)

As can be seen from this passage the notion of alienation is highly abstract and philosophical thereby presenting formidable obstacles to empirical verification. It is, in other works, extremely difficult to determine whether or not a given group of workers is in fact 'alienated'.

Blauner attempts to 'operationalise' alienation, that is, transpose the concept into a testable form by breaking it down into four subvariables: *powerlessness*, referring to the worker's lack of control over decision-making, conditions of employment and the immediate work process; *meaninglessness*, arising out of the division of labour and job standardisation, leading to job fragmentation and an inability to identify with the whole product; *isolation*, referring to a lack of integration into work groups; and *self-estrangement*, a condition in which work is external, not part of oneself, simply a means to satisfy other needs.

Having identified the components of alienation Blauner proceeds to formulate sets of questions along each dimension which are then used in interviews with groups of workers in different industries. The industries selected are craft printing, textile manufacture, automobile manufacture and automated chemical production. These industries are selected deliberately as symptomatic of stages in the process of industrialisation: craft printing, a pre-industrial occupation which survived into the industrial era; textile manufacture being an industry we associate with the early 'take-off' stage of industrialisation; automobile assembly being typical of mature capitalism – the stage of 'high mass consumption'; and last, automated continuous process production representing a highly advanced stage of industrialisation: in effect the future.

It needs to be clear that, although alienation is central to his study, Blauner is not a Marxist. On the contrary he is attempting to steer a course between what he sees as two extremes: on the one hand a dogmatic Marxism which considers *all* work under capitalism to be alienated labour; and, on the other, the bland optimism of a Human Relations approach which believes that simple social engineering can dispense with problems in the work situation. Blauner does not dispute that work under capitalism may have powerful alienating tendencies, but believes that this varies a good deal with the type of technology. This is borne out by his findings which reveal that the degree of alienation measured over the four subvariables is low in craft printing, increases in textile manufacture, reaches a peak in automobile assembly but then declines rapidly under automated chemical production. The high levels of skill associated with craft printing give that occupation interest, autonomy, status and a favourable degree of security. Craft printing, like most skilled trades, it is also associated with a strong sense of occupational solidarity. Alienation is therefore low on all four dimensions. Work tasks in textile manufacture, that is, machine-minding technology, are fragmented, embody low levels of skill, yield little satisfaction and have low status. However, textile manufacture is associated with integrated occupational communities – the mill towns with their high levels of social interaction amongst family and workmates. Accordingly whilst alienation for this occupation is high on powerlessness, meaninglessness and self-estrangement, it is low on the isolation variable. Assembly-line work is not only unskilled (therefore insecure) and extremely boring, but also offers minimal scope for social interaction both inside and outside the plant. Whereas textile workers live and work close together, the typical car worker drives home along to his urban housing estate (Goldthorpe *et al.*'s 'privatised' worker; see Chapter 4). Alienation is at a peak. However, when we come to the automated chemical plant, the nature of the technology – essentially involving the supervision of self-regulating processes – frees the operative from constant pressure, emphasising variety and responsibility in the workplace. Continuous process technology also requires teamwork which in turn promotes social integration. A strong market for this plant's products ensure a stable employment situation. Alienation is low on all four dimensions (see Table 7.1).

Like all sociological studies Blauner's should in no sense be taken as the last word. It has been the target of numerous criticisms, some of which will be touched on later in this and the succeeding chapter. For the time being we should note the optimistic conclusion of his research (as we shall see by no means confined to Blauner's work). This is that, although mass production appears to have brought about a crisis in terms of high levels of alienation, once we get beyond this stage of development the future looks a lot brighter. In other words, as the process of industrialisation unfolds, the level of dissatisfaction and discontent at work is *not* doomed progressively to increase. This finding is interesting not least because it runs against a fairly dominant line of thought which takes a much more pessimistic view. The 'deskilling' hypothesis is implicit in the work of a number of writers

Table 7.1 Degree of alienation by industry

Type of industry Type of technology	**Printing** **Craft**	**Textiles** **Machine-** **minding**	**Automobiles** **Mass** **Production** **(Assembly Line)**	**Chemicals** **Continuous** **Process**
DEGREE OF ALIENATION				
1. Powerlessness	LOW	HIGH	HIGH	LOW
2. Meaninglessness	LOW	HIGH	HIGH	LOW
3. Isolation	LOW	LOW	HIGH	LOW
4. Self-estrangement	LOW	HIGH	HIGH	LOW

Source: J. E. T. Eldridge (1971) *Sociology and Industrial Life* (London : Michael Joseph).

going back at least to Max Weber. However it was given a very coherent and forceful restatement in the seventies with the appearance of Harry Braverman's *Labour and Monopoly Capital: The Degradation of Work in the Twentieth Century* (1974).

BRAVERMAN AND DESKILLING

Braverman (1920–76) trained as a skilled coppersmith and worked in a variety of industrial locations where he was able to observe the effects of changing technology on craft skills. In later years as a journalist and book publisher he also became conscious of the impact of modern technology on administrative areas such as accounting, management and distribution as well as on book production. In his *Labour and Monopoly Capital* Braverman develops the thesis that there is a deep-rooted tendency for work under capitalism to be deskilled as more and more expertise and knowledge is transferred from the worker to management.

As a Marxist Braverman employs Marx's term 'labour process' to refer to the ways in which raw materials are transformed into commodities through the use of machines and tools. In a capitalist system these machines and tools are owned by the capitalists who pay property-less workers a wage to produce goods for profit. Under this system it is essential, according to Braverman, that the owners 'exploit' the workers in the sense of obtaining as much as out of their labour as they can whilst paying them as little as possible in return. This means that in an era dominated by large corporations (monopoly capitalism), managers, as the principal agents of the owners, must constantly seek to redesign and modify the labour process in order to achieve maximum profit. To reach this goal management needs to assert as much control over the labour force as possible. This is accomplished by dividing (fragmenting) the process of production into a large number of extremely simple tasks with the complete process firmly under central control. Management is thereby able to achieve higher levels of output from a labour force which, because it is less skilled, is considerably cheaper as well as more easily replaced.

The prime advocate of this type of approach to the organisation of production is F. W. Taylor, whose scientific management Braverman sees as providing the rationale for controlling labour in the capitalist enterprise. The core of Taylorism advocates precisely this breaking down of production into its smallest possible units and then, by means of such devices as the time study, carefully controlling the speed at which each operation is completed. Wherever possible worker autonomy is restricted and jobs redesigned in order to transfer knowledge, discretion and hence control to management. As a result traditional distinctions between skilled and unskilled labour are in the process of disappearing as work becomes increasingly fragmented and routinised – in short, deskilled. It is important to appreciate that this 'degradation' of work affects not just manual occupations. Braverman devotes a considerable amount of time to showing how an increasing range of clerical and administrative jobs are being deskilled as a result of the introduction of advanced technology. This leads him to claim that the long-established distinction between manual and non-manual labour is also in the process of being eroded.

This general reduction of work to a few simple and repetitive tasks is held to have had the undesirable consequence of rendering it unrewarding, meaningless and ultimately dehumanising. It is no coincidence, suggests Braverman, that the expansion of large-scale production in the United States coincided with the growth of industrial psychology as a discipline and its increasing application to the selection and training of workers. In other words psychology and after Hawthorne, sociology, were harnessed to the task of habituating an unenthusiastic labour force to the world of mass production. Nonetheless, the new social sciences, Braverman maintains, played only a minor role in the process of adaptation. Rather he places the emphasis on socioeconomic conditions and forces. The development of mass production in the automobile industry is used by Braverman to illustrate not only how American labour was persuaded to accept the new world of work, but in addition his underlying theme of the transition from craft production to machine-paced mass production.

SOME COMMENTS ON BRAVERMAN

Braverman's deskilling thesis obviously runs directly contrary to the conclusions of Blauner's research. It also conflicts with the ideas of the Industrial Society theorists referred to in Chapter 4. Far from deskilling, writers such as Ralf Dahrendorf and Clark Kerr believed that as industrialisation proceeds the demand for skilled labour must increase. As technology grows more complex, more qualified designers, builders, engineers, maintenance and repair personnel are needed. How might we evaluate these apparently contradictory claims?

First, it is crucial to appreciate that it is actually quite difficult to distinguish between skilled and less skilled occupations. There is, for example, no universally accepted objective definition of skilled work. Furthermore, the fact that a given occupation is currently designated 'skilled' does not necessarily mean that its practitioners are engaged in work that is more skilled than others labelled 'semi-skilled' or 'unskilled'. It can mean that the 'skilled craftsman' has in the past served an apprenticeship, is a member of a union and that the union has been able to sustain skilled rates of pay even though most of the traditional skills associated with that craft have been rendered redundant by technological advance. It is thus not unusual, during times of rapid change, to find two individuals doing the same job, yet for one of them to be classified as skilled, the other semi-skilled. If we look at the manual sector in Britain, occupations categorised as skilled are overwhelmingly male and invariably strongly unionised. Many occupations in which females predominate, for example, electronics assembly and the garment trade, require considerable manual dexterity but are seldom regarded as skilled. This is not, of course, to argue that designated 'skilled' occupations entail no skill at all, simply that behind what often seem to be objective 'facts' lie complex social and economic processes. These observations need to be borne in mind when we examine official statistics relating to the changing skill composition of the labour force.

In addition to the complications mentioned above, official statistics, unfortunately, do not help us to reach any unequivocal conclusion. In fact the figures in Table 7.2 could be taken to support both deskilling and reskilling hypotheses. We see from the table that the proportion of both skilled and semi-skilled workers declined by more than 7 per cent over the 30-year period. However, we note that we do not encounter a significant increase in the unskilled category as Marxist-inspired theories would lead

Table 7.2 Distribution of Britain's economically active population, 1951 and 1981, by occupational category (percentages)

	1951	*1981*
Employers and self-employed	6.7	6.4
Managers and administrators	5.4	10.1
Professionals and technicians	6.6	14.7
Clerical and sales	16.3	19.3
Supervisors and foremen	2.6	4.2
Skilled manual	23.8	16.0
Semi-skilled manual	26.6	19.0
Unskilled manual	11.9	10.4

Source: Table 3.3 in C. Hamnett, L. McDowell and P. Sarr (eds) (1989) *The Changing Social Structure* (London: Sage).

us to expect. On the contrary there is a slight decrease of 1.5 per cent. This highlights the fact that the proportion employed in manual occupations as a whole declined over this period. Accordingly it is difficult to conclude how much of the decline in skilled manual occupations is attributable to deskilling or to a more fundamental disappearance of manual jobs generally. We will have more to say about the latter in the next chapter. Let us first of all note the significant increase in the proportion of managers and administrators and professionals and technicians – the latter more than doubling over our period. Does this not give strong support to the *reskilling* argument? The answer is that it may, but once again we need to be aware of the social complexities that lie behind what appear to be simple labels.

In fact it is very difficult to reach a satisfactory definition of a 'profession'. For this reason sociologists prefer to concern themselves with 'professionalisation', the social process under which occupations seek to improve their standing in the public eye (Box 7.1). Accordingly, to term an occupation a profession may tell us more about the aspirations of its practitioners than about the degree of skill involved in its performance. Indeed an upsurge in professional consciousness may actually coincide with some loss of skill, especially in terms of declining autonomy. It has been observed that professional and technical workers, together with lower levels of management, often become exceedingly preoccupied with their professional status precisely when it is under threat, usually through the imposition of increased bureaucratic control. In other words, a statistical increase in the number/proportion of professional and technical occupations is not incompatible with the deskilling thesis. That is to say, the number of occupations which *lay claim* to professional or special technical status may be growing, but the labour process in which they are involved may be increasingly subject to deskilling pressures as a result of technological change and/or intensifying competition. This would seem to suggest that in order to evaluate the deskilling hypothesis adequately we need to look beyond statistics at the labour process itself. In fact the qualitative data that is available on non-manual occupations would seem to lend a good deal of support to the notion of deskilling.

Box 7.1 Professions and professionalisation

Most definitions of a 'profession' are based upon the long-established professions, mainly medicine and the law. These are occupations which traditionally have sold their intellectual services for a fee and whose professional associations have served as a guarantee of reliability. Because of their generally high status in society, other occupations have sought to emulate the established professions. This is a process –

professionalisation – in which the occupation or area of business seeks to persuade the public/employers that the services/skills of its practitioners are the genuine article, can be relied upon, can be trusted. This invariably requires the setting up of a professional association which registers members who are suitably qualified, the implication being that non-members should be regarded with caution. During the property boom of the late eighties, for example, the (British) National Association of Estate Agents became extremely concerned about the bad publicity the profession was attracting owing to the dubious practices of a minority of unscrupulous operators. Accordingly, the NAEA was pressing the Government to introduce tighter controls over who could practise as an estate agent. (At that time Britain was one of the few European countries where no qualifications were needed to set up as an estate agent). The basic aim of the NAEA, like that of other professional associations, is to persuade members of the public or employers that the services of its members can be relied upon, are 'professional'.

THE DESKILLING OF NON-MANUAL WORK

A number of studies of routine clerical staff have revealed that the work of this sector has been increasingly affected by mechanisation since the beginning of the century. In a much-quoted study published in 1958, David Lockwood indicated the extent to which routine white-collar work was subject to deskilling with the introduction of adding machines, addressographs and other mechanised systems (Lockwood, *The Blackcoated Worker*, Allen & Unwin). Latterly such occupations have felt the impact of computer technology which seems to have accelerated significantly well-established deskilling tendencies. This is effectively demonstrated by an extremely useful piece of research on clerical workers in a local authority treasurer's department carried out by Rosemary Crompton and Stuart Reid. Here the whole process of clerical work is now geared to the computer. Information on the pay of council employees comes in from the various departments on standard forms. The data is transferred onto a payroll card (one for each employee) which is then sent to the computer department where it is transferred to disk or tape. The computer produces a print-out which is checked for errors by the clerk who, after making necessary corrections, submits the data for a final run. The computer then produces a payslip and a cheque for each employee.

There can be no doubt that computerisation has dramatically increased the capacity of this department to handle large volumes of data with great speed and accuracy. But in the process the clerk's role has been diminished; virtually reduced to making corrections and alterations. Crompton and

Reid found that staff frequently expressed feelings of dependence, of subordination to the computer. For those employees who had worked for the council for some years and had had experience of the pre-computer era, the transformation was particularly striking: the element of personal contact had gone; the specialised knowledge that was needed to deal with a range of problems was now redundant. One section head complained of the difficulties of motivating staff when work followed an interminable pattern 'almost like a conveyor belt'.

The value of the clerk to the employer once resided in the detailed knowledge which made up what Crompton and Reid term the 'clerical craft'. In addition clerks often exercised some supervisory authority on behalf of their employers. Both aspects of the clerical role have been seriously eroded. The clerk is now typically virtually the appendage of a machine, the computer, with little responsibility for the coordination of separate work tasks or for their final 'product'. The introduction of computers has increased the centralisation of authority in the department, one of the main consequences of which has been the relocation of the supervisory function to higher levels of management. A corollary of the deskilling of clerical labour is its transformation into predominantly female work. For example, the authors found that the operators who transferred the data from standard forms to disks or tape were exclusively female, engaged in what amounted to a highly repetitive machine-minding job. With the development of this type of situation – a situation which, Crompton and Reid maintain, is by no means confined to their own sample of white-collar workers – the once clearly-marked boundary between non-manual and manual labour all but disappears.

Given that most routine white-collar work has long ceased to be specialised, has become precisely 'routine', these findings are probably not so surprising. They represent merely the speeding up of a long-established trend. With more specialised occupations – those that fit unequivocally into the 'professional and technical' category – the impact of computerisation has been much more dramatic. This is well brought out by Mike Cooley, an engineer and trade unionist, who looks at the way certain engineering specialisms are being transformed. Take the draughtsman for example: until the forties he (yet again it was invariably 'he') was at the centre of design activity. The draughtsman would design a component, draw it, stress it out and specify the material and the quantities of lubrication needed. Nowadays each of these tasks has been divided between a number of separate specialisms: the designer designs, the draughtsman draws, the metallurgist specifies the materials, the stress analyst the structure and the tribologist the lubrication. But not only has the labour process been fragmented; the now separate areas within it are being radically changed by the new technology. Formerly the draughtsman, having produced his drawings, had then to work closely with the skilled craftsmen on the shop floor to iron out any difficulties. What the draughtsman does now is to input details of the drawing he wants into a computer which produces a design on tape. The tape can then be used to operate directly some piece of engineering equipment such as a jig borer or a milling machine, including doing its own inspecting and correcting. With these developments not only has the interaction between draughtsman and craftsman disappeared but also the craftsmen themselves!

Cooley uses this and other examples to highlight the extent to which specialised knowledge is being abstracted from individuals and embedded in organisations. In fact he sees the computer as the 'Trojan Horse' through which Taylorism is being introduced into intellectual work. One view of computerisation, as we have seen, is that it will free human beings from routine, soul-destroying and backbreaking tasks, leaving them free to engage in more creative work. Cooley questions this assumption, maintaining that the same deskilling processes that have been eroding craft work over the past century are increasingly degrading mental labour.

Taking into account these and other pieces of research, there seems to be a fair amount of support for the deskilling thesis. Whether this deskilling is the result of a conscious application (*à la* Braverman) of Taylorism or more the inevitable consequence of the seemingly perpetual drive for greater efficiency need not trouble us at this point. More important for the moment are the implications. An examination of the long-term consequences of the general displacement of jobs by technology – Cooley's disappearing shop-floor craftsmen – we must leave until the final chapter. Let us look at the more immediate effects of deskilling for the world of work. Does this mean that an increasing number of adults, perhaps a majority in advanced capitalist societies, are constrained to spend half their lives engaged in an activity that requires minimal skill, is repetitive and dull and yields negligible intrinsic satisfaction? If this is indeed the case, what are the consequences for the individual, for management, for the firm, for society at large?

ARE WE HAPPY IN OUR WORK?

A short answer to the above question could be an emphatic 'yes'. Surveys carried out in Europe and the United States indicate a high level of professed satisfaction with work. In Britain for example, the government-run General Household Survey 1974 reported that 85 per cent of its respondents were 'very satisfied' or 'fairly satisfied' with their jobs. Only 3 per cent described themselves as 'very dissatisfied'. How are we to interpret such findings in the light of the research into the effects of deskilling? We could simply accept them at face value and conclude that work for most of us is not a problem. However, a significant number of studies of the workplace itself suggest that we should be cautious about reaching such a conclusion. Like all replies to survey questions such responses are susceptible of various interpretations. They might, for example, be symptomatic of an unwillingness to admit to overall dissatisfaction because of the centrality of work in our type of society. Since work is a core human activity and therefore very much part of our identity, to admit to finding it meaningless might seem to amount to an acknowledgement of personal failure. Alternatively apparently high levels of overall satisfaction might mean that whilst some aspects of a job are unrewarding, in general you are not unhappy with it. It may be the case that people will put up with boring and repetitive work so long as the wages are high enough. Studies of car assembly workers in the United States and Britain suggest that this may be the case. In the 1960s J. H. Goldthorpe investigated the attitudes and behaviour of car workers in Luton. Corroborating many other studies of this industry Goldthorpe finds that these workers derive little intrinsic satisfaction from their work, generally finding it boring and repetitive. Yet they did not express overall dissatisfaction with the jobs they were doing. One of the most important and interesting findings of this piece of research is that most of the workers expected the job to be boring before they came to it. However they were prepared to put up with its deprivations for the sake of high wages. In fact a sizeable proportion of the men in the sample (38 per cent) had spent the greater part of their working lives before becoming car assemblers in higher-status, more skilled (and probably more intrinsically satisfying) jobs. The main point that Goldthorpe is making is that this *instrumental* orientation of work – one that we encountered in Chapter 4 – is something the assembler brings with him/her to the job and is *not* a consequence of the job itself, that is, of the type of technology employed. Goldthorpe and others have seen in this situation – one in which we work not for the sake of working but in order to satisfy other (consumptionist) needs – the essence of Marx's notion of alienation.

Whether or not 'alienation' appropriately describes the condition of even a majority of those engaged in full-time employment is a highly complex issue which cannot be resolved here. The point is that despite low levels of expressed dissatisfaction there is enough evidence to support the proposition that for a significant proportion of employees the character of work in industrial society presents problems, especially problems of motivation.

This evidence, it is important to appreciate, comes not only from research carried out by social scientists, but increasingly from the attitudes and policies adopted by management and governments throughout the industrial capitalist world. The widespread introduction of Taylorite methods had certainly made possible massive rises in production whilst at the same time achieving a considerable reduction in labour costs. But against these gains needs to be offset a number of undesirable side-effects. As mass-production methods were disseminated throughout Europe and the United States, management was more and more constrained to recognise that they tended to be associated with such pathologies as absenteeism, high labour turnover, a high level of industrial disputes, shoddy work and, not infrequently, sabotage. (See Box 7.2.) Since all of these represent costs for the enterprise then there comes a point at which the pursuit of policies directed at countering the undesirable consequences of modern production methods becomes an economic necessity.

Box 7.2 Industrial sabotage

Absenteeism, high labour turnover, strikes, overtime bans and output restrictions are familiar expressions of worker discontent. Equally important but usually less visible is industrial sabotage. Whilst sometimes employed as a conscious strategy, sabotage is more frequently a spontaneous outburst against oppressive work conditions. For many writers the very unpredictability and apparent irrationality of sabotage makes it the most damaging form of protest. The following examples are drawn from research carried out by two English sociologists (L. Taylor and P. Walton):

> They had to throw away half a mile of Blackpool rock last year, for, instead of the customary motif running through its length, it carried the terse injunction 'Fuck Off'...In the Christmas rush in a Knightsbridge store the machine which shuttled change backwards and forwards suddenly ground to a halt. A frustrated salesman had demobilized it by ramming a cream bun down its gullet...Railwaymen have described how they block lines with trucks to delay shunting operations a few hours. Materials are hidden in factories, conveyor belts jammed with sticks...lorries 'accidentally' backed into ditches.

Taylor and Walton go on to relate how steel workers, knowing steel slabs to be too cold for rolling, nonetheless allowed them to proceed on to the rollers where the steel would undoubtedly be ruined. 'They make the decisions, we couldn't care less', was the view of the steel workers. American studies have revealed how car workers sabotage their products by deliberately sealing banana skins or tin cans into car bodies.

(Examples taken from K. Kumar (1978) *Prophecy and Progress*.)

JOB ENRICHMENT

In recent years management in both private and public sectors has shown
an increasing interest in programmes of job enrichment. In the early seventies the French government created a post of Minister of Job Enrichment.
In 1973 Britain's Department of Employment published a report, *On the
Quality of Working Life*, which summarised case studies of people's work
experiences in four countries, including the United Kingdom. The main
thrust of the report was to highlight what it saw as the overemphasis by
senior managers on levels of production and the corresponding neglect of
the impact of work on the general quality of life of the labour force. The
publication of the report led to the setting up of the Work Research Unit
and the Tripartite Steering Committee on Job Satisfaction. The prime
function of the WRU (formerly part of the Department of Employment,
now under the auspices of the Advisory, Conciliation and Arbitration Service) is to conduct research into the impact of job redesign programmes
and to disseminate the findings. The Tripartite Steering Committee is
chaired by a minister of state and includes representatives from both the
Trades Union Congress and the Confederation of British Industry. Its main
task is to advise the Secretary of State for Employment on how to
encourage employers and trade unions to take action to improve the job
satisfaction of employees.

But quite independently of government action there are numerous examples of large employers throughout the industrialised world who have taken
the initiative to introduce their own job enrichment programmes. One of
the most often cited examples is that of the Swedish car and truck manufacturer, Volvo. Faced with high labour turnover in the sixties Volvo management embarked upon an ambitious programme to increase motivation and
job satisfaction. A key feature of the programme was the creation of small
workgroups which were given responsibility for a complete subsection of a
vehicle's construction, for example, truck cab, brakes and wheels. The size
of each workgroup varied from between three and twelve depending upon
the task in hand. Tasks were allocated a few days in advance with group
members given responsibility for organising production and dividing work
between themselves. Each group elected a leader who became its spokes-
man and liaised with foremen and production engineers. In many areas *job
rotation* was introduced, giving individuals the opportunity to move
through several different work tasks from assembly work to inspection.

In 1974 Volvo took a much more radical step, constructing an entirely
new plant at Kalmar (Sweden) where assembly-line production was abolished altogether. Here the assembly of each vehicle was broken down into

twenty different functions each performed by teams of fifteen to twenty workers. Vehicles in the process of being assembled are moved from team to team on rubber-wheeled electrically driven trolleys. Whilst teams are obliged to meet certain production norms, it is up to members to organise the cycle for which they are responsible. The group conducts its own inspection which is monitored by a television screen at their work station. Low levels of noise allow employees to talk to each other and even to listen to music. Overall the improved working environment, the greater worker autonomy and higher level of involvement that the team system permits have substantially enhanced the quality of working life at Kalmar. These innovations are claimed to have made possible significant increases in production – 20 per cent higher than the goal set for the project – as well as reducing labour turnover to 16 per cent (50 per cent in 'normal' Volvo plants). Volvo has since extended the Kalmar system to many of its other plants. In 1988 at a new facility at Uddevalla (Sweden) teams of seven to ten workers were given the responsibility for the complete assembly of four cars per shift. Because work-team members are trained to handle all assembly jobs, they work an average of three hours before repeating the same task. The comparable figure for a standard assembly line in Detroit (United States) is 1.5 minutes. At Uddevalla both employee morale and product quality are up. Absenteeism at 8 per cent compares very favourably with the industry average of 20 per cent. Labour turnover is also well below industry norms.

The Volvo example is not untypical of the hundreds of job redesign programmes that have been implemented throughout the industrialised world. Saab, Fiat, Olivetti, IBM, Singer, American Telephone and Telegraph, General Motors, Texas Instruments, as well as most large Japanese firms, are a few of the large corporations which have introduced programmes of this nature. It needs to be made clear that the restructuring of work may simply entail *job enlargement* where the number of operations is increased, or *job rotation* where the employee moves through a series of tasks according to a given sequence. The main point is that both job enlargement and job rotation involve an expansion in the scope of work but *within the same overall level of skill*. That is to say, the increased number of operations or jobs does not entail an enhancement of skills. Job enrichment, by contrast, is invariably held to increase the level of skill, to give workers greater responsibility and ultimately greater control over the labour process. This last is extremely important as it embodies an apparent reversal of Taylorism with its central precept that workers merely 'do' whilst managers 'plan'. This shift is in line with much current management thinking which seems to favour movement away from the authoritarian management style implicit in Taylorism to more participative forms. The two polar types are embodied in a very influential model proposed by former corporate executive Douglas McGregor. As a result of many years' experience in business, McGregor was led to propose (in 1960) that a manager's approach to managing flows directly from whatever theory of human behaviour he/she holds. McGregor goes on to outline two basic sets of assumptions which he terms Theory X and Theory Y

As can be seen from Box 7.3, Theory X entails the assumption that most people dislike work and will try and avoid it if possible. They engage in various subterfuges, have little ambition, will avoid responsibility and obstruct change. The incentives and rewards offered by the organisation are unable to overcome the dislike for work. Accordingly the only way in which management can obtain high productivity is to increase control, coerce and threaten.

Theory Y assumes that people are not inherently lazy. They may seem to be lazy but this is a reaction to the way the organisations have been run in the past. In other words management has generally subscribed to Theory X and acted accordingly. In this way Theory X is a self-fulfilling prophecy: treating people as feckless and uncooperative creates the conditions which encourage them to be so. If managers will but provide the proper organisational setting employees will exercise self-control, become self-directed, and will be able to realise their potential in the pursuit of organisational goals. Obviously Theory Y assumptions will give rise to more participative

Box 7.3 Theory X and Theory Y

Theory X	Theory Y
The typical person dislikes work and will avoid it if possible.	Work is as natural as rest.
The typical person lacks responsibility, has little ambition and values security above all.	People are not inherently lazy although they may appear so.
Most people must be coerced, controlled and threatened with punishment to get them to work.	People will exercise self-direction and self-control under appropriate conditions.
	People have potential imagination and creativity – and can learn to seek and accept responsibility.

Source: D. McGregor (1960) *The Human Side of Enterprise* (New York: McGraw-Hill).

and flexible styles of management. However, on the question of participation it is important to distinguish between *levels* of participation. Participation can, after all, run from employees being occasionally consulted about management decisions to the kind of highly institutionalised participation in executive decision-making that exists in some European countries. This latter has been termed *power-centred* participation and is best illustrated by the German system of codetermination.

Codetermination was adopted in the then Republic of West Germany as part of the restructuring and de-Nazifying of German labour relations after the Second World War. The basic principle underlying it is that workers have a right to participate in the running of the firms they work for. The forms codetermination takes vary from industry to industry. In the coal and steel industries employees elect over half the members of supervisory boards with shareholders electing the other half. Worker representatives in these industries are effectively able to nominate the firm's labour director who is responsible for personnel issues. Outside coal and steel, workers elect one-third of board members. In all German industries works councils elected by employees have the right to 'codetermine' certain issues, mainly working hours, holidays and the implementation of pay scales; to veto certain others – hiring, job classification and transfers; and to be consulted over others, for example, mass redundancies and individual dismissals. Works councils also have the right to receive certain information relating to profits, investment and the like. Despite these formal provisions the degree of worker influence over company affairs is thought to be limited. Outside coal and steel boards, workers are in a minority which means that they can always be outvoted by employers and shareholder representatives. In addition the flow of information is restricted and the right to use it even more so. Employee representatives are bound by rules of confidentiality not to disclose certain information. This severely limits their ability to mobilise the labour force against radical changes.

Works councils similar to those in Germany also exist in France and Belgium. However, in Britain there is no statutory requirement regarding worker participation and neither of the two main political parties has expressed support for such legislation. On the contrary the Conservative Party, especially during the Thatcher era, was resolutely opposed to the 'democratisation-of-economic-life' ethos that emanates from the European Commission and which is embodied in the Social Chapter.

The impetus behind *power-centred* participation is precisely the question of power and a conviction that a full-fledged democracy cannot be said to exist unless the principle of meaningful participation is extended to the workplace. *Power-centred* participation has been contrasted with *task-centred* participation. The impetus behind the latter springs from a management concern with efficiency and quality and has little to do with questions of power and democracy. *Task-centred* participation, is seen as a means of countering the pathological effects of mass production by increasing employee autonomy and responsibility at work – in short, job enrichment. There can be little doubt that a good deal of the impetus behind the distinct shift over the past two decades to more task-centred forms of work organisation derives from the Japanese experience. Japan's stupendous economic success over the past 25 years has prompted European and American management gurus to look closely at Japanese management. One of the core features of Japanese management seems to be the Quality Circle. Although they originated in the United States, Quality Circles were exported to Japan and from the early sixties were widely adopted in manufacturing and in some areas of white-collar employment. A Quality Circle comprises a group of people within an organisation who meet together on a regular basis to identify, analyse and solve problems concerning quality, productivity or any other aspects of the day-to-day arrangements of working life. The membership of Quality Circles is voluntary and they usually consist of five to ten individuals engaged in broadly similar work. Although they are usually led by a first-line supervisor, the problem to be analysed is selected by the group and recommendations made to management. Very large claims are made for Quality Circles: at ITT, according to Quality guru, Philip B. Crosby, they are supposed to have saved 720 million dollars in a year. (*Quality is Free*, Mentor, 1988). In Britain one of the leading enthusiasts is Wedgwood where around one hundred Circles of about ten workers each are in operation. These have been able to make numerous recommendations for improving the organisation of production, increasing efficiency and enhancing quality. Industrial relations have also been improved and a greater sense of involvement in the firm stimulated. Rolls-Royce, IBM, Duracell and British Telecom have also used Quality Circles with similar claimed success.

CONCLUSION

As a general conceptualisation of the age of high mass consumption – the Fordist era – Braverman's basic theme of the degradation of labour is appealing. Certainly there can be little doubt that the growth in the scale of production has required a significant increase in organisational complexity which in turn has demanded an extreme division of labour with the breaking down of work tasks into ever simpler sets of operations.

This is not the place to engage in a detailed critique of Braverman's argument. Nonetheless, two basic points relating to it need to be made. First, it is not the case that even a bare majority in pre-industrial/early industrial society were engaged in craft production. Work for most people during these periods comprised the unrewarding and at best partly skilled drudgery of the agricultural and town labourer. Furthermore, we must also bear in mind that life for the majority of the population of industrial societies well into this century was characterised by long periods of unemployment and under-employment and the kind of poverty that we now associate with the third world. Conversely we need to be aware that even at the height of the Fordist era – the early sixties for example – most employees did not work on assembly lines but drove buses, built houses, served in shops, taught in schools or worked in hospitals or the civil service and so forth. In other works the basic theme of a fundamental shift from fulfilling craft work to alienating assembly-line production needs to be treated with caution.

Despite these reservations there is a considerable body of evidence which supports the thesis of the generally negative consequences of the growth in the scale of production for the experience of work. Not only is this evidence to be found in the work of social scientists such as Cooley and Crompton and Reid, as well as in the studies carried out by such bodies as the Work Research Unit, but more importantly, in the growing recognition by many large employers of the need for some kind of restructuring of the work situation. A major feature of such restructuring would seem to be a shift towards more participative forms of management together with its corollary: some degree of transfer of autonomy and expertise from formal organisation back to employees – in a word, 'reskilling'. The main point is that were such a shift to be generally under way we would be witnessing not simply a reversal of the impact of decades of Taylorism, but a major transformation in the character of industrial society itself. Indeed we could even be transcending the industrial era and entering a radically different phase in the development of human society. In effect, the main focus of our next chapter will be upon the question of the character and extent of such fundamental changes as are taking place.

BIBLIOGRAPHY

Beynon, H. (1984) *Working For Ford* (Harmondsworth: Penguin).
Braverman, H. (1974) *Labour and Monopoly Capital* (New York: Monthly Review Press).
Burns, T. (ed.) (1969) *Industrial Man* (Harmondsworth: Penguin).

Cooley, M. (1989) 'Computers and the Mechanisation of Intellectual Work', in G. Morgan (ed.), *Creative Organisation Theory* (London: Sage).

Crompton, R. and Reid, S. (1982) 'The deskilling of clerical work', in S. Wood (ed.), *The Degradation of Work?* (London: Hutchinson).

Eldridge, J. E. T. (1971) *Sociology and Industrial Life* (London: Michael Joseph).

Goldthorpe, J. H. (1966) 'Attitudes and Behaviour of Car Assembly Workers', *British Journal of Sociology*, vol. 17.

Hamnett, C., McDowell, L. and Sarre, P. (eds) (1989) *The Changing Social Structure* (London: Sage).

Kumar, K. (1978) *Prophecy and Progress* (London: Allen Lane).

Littler, C. R. (1986) *The Development of the Labour Process in Capitalist Societies* (Aldershot: Gower).

McLellan, D. (1971) *The Thought of Karl Marx* (London: Macmillan).

Mullins, L. J. (1989) *Management and Organisational Behaviour* (London: Pitman).

Pugh, D. S. and Hickson, D. J. (1989) *Writers on Organisations* (Harmondsworth: Penguin).

Terkel, S. (1977) *Working* (Harmondsworth: Penguin).

Thompson, P. (1983) *The Nature of Work* (London: Macmillan).

Thompson, P. and McHugh, D. (1990) *Work Organisations* (London: Macmillan).

8 Beyond Industrial Society?

The main theme of this book is that industrialisation is a highly complex process which has moved through and continues to move through a number of discernible phases. Integral to this theme is the view that these phases can be adequately understood only in the perspective of an ever-changing world economy. Industrialisation refers not simply to the harnessing of new sources of power and new technologies to the production of goods and services. The diffusion of industrialism has had far-reaching consequences for the whole of social life. Industrialisation eventually created a 'modern' society, – that is, a society which went beyond providing basic necessities for the bulk of its citizens – to reach a stage where ever higher levels of consumption came to be seen as a reasonable and legitimate expectation.

For Industrial Society theorists such as Kerr and Dahrendorf the attainment of the stage of high mass consumption marked a crucial phase in the process of industrialisation. As far as they were concerned the ability of Industrial Society to provide most of its citizens with a decent and improving standard of living was of pivotal significance in defusing the often intense social conflict with which such societies had been plagued for more than a century and a half. Furthermore, the high level of consumption was not just a happy accident but a necessary outcome of the 'logic of industrialism': the outworking of scientific rationality as it expresses itself in the process of production and in social institutions generally. If the path of industrialism is determined by some internal scientific logic then it follows that if human beings were to acquire a sound understanding of this logic then they could predict and plan the course of social change. This is, in fact, the view of Industrial Society theorists: scientific knowledge can be harnessed to both production and social organisation to produce an orderly 'rational' society – in essence a condition which approximates closely to the society of 'order and progress' which pioneering sociologist August Comte believed that correct social scientific planning would eventually produce.

The Industrial Society outlook appeared in the late fifties and early sixties, by no means accidentally, at the height of the post war boom. Although by the early seventies boom was being superseded by recession the belief among some social scientists in the possibility of a 'rational' society remains unshaken. However, in the seventies the thesis was restated in a somewhat amended from which proposed the emergence from within the womb of industrial society of a *post-industrial* society. The central thrust behind the post-industrial society argument is the growing preponderance of the services sector in the economies of developed societies. If we look at Britain for example we note that the proportion of the labour force working in services increased by almost 20 per cent over the period 1960 to 1980 (from 45 to 62 per cent). Some have speculated that by the turn of the century 80 per cent of the labour force could be working in services. The main point is that if we take the essential feature of an industrial society to be the manufacture of material goods, then by the mid-eighties less than one-quarter of the labour force was engaged in this type of activity. Looked at in another way, it seems that manufacturing's contribution to Britain's gross domestic product has been steadily declining for a considerable period, with services accounting for more than half of domestic production since the 1960s. It needs to be emphasised that this trend, in varying degree, is observable in all industrial societies, with the United States allegedly having made the transition to a service economy more than a quarter of a century ago.

As we have seen, the shift in the centre of gravity of production from the primary (mainly agriculture) to the secondary (manufacturing) sector brought about revolutionary social changes. So too, the argument goes, will the shift currently under way towards the tertiary (services) sector. Some indication of the character of these changes will be apparent if we look briefly at the arguments of one of the principal proponents of the post-industrial scenario, American sociologist Daniel Bell.

THE IDEA OF A POST-INDUSTRIAL SOCIETY

There is in Bell's basic thesis a considerable degree of continuity with the arguments of the Industrial Society theorists in that underlying both is the notion that some kind of internal logic propels society from one stage to the next. Bell, accordingly, employs the term 'axial principle' to denote the subterranean rationality whose outworking drives society forward. An axial principle is the primary principle from which all other patterns of rational thought flow. Axial structures are the institutions which most strongly express the axial principle. In *industrial* societies the axial principle is economising: that is to say, the optimal allocation of resources. The axial structure of industrial society is the business enterprise. Bell, writing at the end of the sixties, discerns the rise of a new axial principle based upon the centrality of theoretical knowledge. This axial principle expresses itself in institutions which are concerned with the accumulation, codification and transmission of knowledge: universities, research institutes and the like. The idea of the primacy of systematic knowledge has been given a significant boost by the microchip revolution. The diffusion of microprocessing techniques has enormously speeded up the process under which information can be gathered, analysed and applied to the production of a vast range of goods and services, from the use of robots in the production of cars to supermarket checkouts and automatic bank cash dispensers. In fact some writers have sought to promote the idea of an *information* sector either within the services sector or as a fourth sector in its own right. Occupations concerned primarily with handling information, such as teaching, administration, journalism, printing, banking, insurance and the arts, have existed since the early days of industrialism. But the information revolution is producing a situation in which the production of *information as opposed to material goods* is the principal economic activity in contemporary advanced societies. As we move into the next century information will take over as the leading sector and the continuous application of IT will become the primary source of economic growth in the post-industrial era. This means that information handlers and producers, from university researchers to accountants, from systems analysts to publishers, will become post-industrial society's dominant social groups, and knowledge-producing centres will now acquire precedence over the business firm.

Possibly the most radical transformation brought about by the transition to post-industrialism will be in the character of work itself. No more the industrial worker in greasy overalls struggling to keep up with the relentless pace of the machine amidst the grime and clamour of the factory. The typical post-industrial worker sits before a console in an air-conditioned control room feeding commands to a set of computer-controlled milling machines. Or, he/she is the financial consultant faxing sets of figures to a client in Hong Kong from the comfort of his/her tastefully lit and carpeted office. Or, perhaps, the architect closeted in his/her 'electronic cottage' running a set of plans through a computer whose program will instantly identify and correct infringements of building regulations.

In short, work in the post-industrial or information era will be overwhelmingly white-collar with the emphasis on technical and professional skills. Work will also be executed in generally pleasant and amenable surroundings: the office, the research laboratory, the consulting room or the home. It is important to appreciate that a predominant theme in the post-industrial literature is that work will increasingly take place in small units of (mainly knowledge) production. This is because as economic growth continues and incomes rise, a larger proportion is likely to be spent on services, especially personal services – hairdressing, meals in restaurants, holidays, financial and legal services, car and home maintenance and so on. Since personal services have typically been provided by small firms, an overall drift towards the services sector will supposedly generate an increase in the number and significance of small businesses. And, as we saw in Chapter 5, the microchip revolution itself has assisted the prolifera- tion of small firms in at least two respects: information technology allows much greater scope for the cheap and efficient provision of services on a small scale and, second, it reduces administrative overheads.

Overall it seems that work in post-industrial society is no longer a prob- lem. Unrewarding manual labour – the norm for industrial society – is gradually superseded by generally agreeable and intellectually stimulating white-collar work, much of it of a professional character. The large com- plex organisation with its extreme job fragmentation and anonymity slowly gives way to the small firm with its face-to-face social relationships and flexible work patterns. Tensions exist in post-industrial society, particularly tensions between knowledge-elites and the masses. However, the precise planning and policy formulation made possible by the information sector's vastly enhanced knowledge-handling capacity enables conflict at all levels to be regulated and diffused. In essence, post-industrial society is effectively scientific management writ large (see Box 8.1).

Box 8.1 Industrial and post-industrial societies: typical features

Industrial society	Post-industrial society
Manufacturing (secondary sector)	Services (tertiary sector)
Material goods	Knowledge
Blue-collar	White-collar
Working-class	Middle-class
Large units of production	Small units
Bureaucratisation	De-bureaucratisation
Assembly line (Fordism)	Automated/computerised factory or office (post-Fordism)
Job fragmentation (deskilling)	Job enrichment (reskilling)
Taylorism/Theory X management	Theory Y/Theory Z*
*Theory Z is explained in Box 8.2	

In considering the above, however, it should be pointed out that some post- industrial scenarios are a good deal more pessimistic than that outlined so far. Whereas conflict – especially that of long-standing between bureaucratic rationality and individual creativity – certainly has a place in Bell's formulation, for French writer Alain Touraine it is absolutely central. Touraine is in agreement with Industrial Society theorists such as Dahrendorf to the extent that conflict in contemporary industrial society is now divorced from the issue of ownership of the means of production. For Touraine, power and authority now lie in the hands of technocrats, the managers of huge organisations in both public and private sectors. These are the planners, the programmers whose access to and control of knowledge allows them to achieve political dominance over the masses. The latter – the 'programmed' – are relatively powerless to question, let alone resist, the tide of bureaucratic regulation which threatens to engulf them. In emphasising the fundamental conflict between a society dominated by vast impersonal bureaucracies and the question of individual autonomy, Touraine is restating, in a mid-century context, the modern dilemma highlighted by Max Weber fifty years before (Alain Touraine (1974) *The Post-Industrial Society*, New York, Random House).

POST-INDUSTRIAL SOCIETY: AN EVALUATION

Clearly the post-industrial thesis rests heavily on the notion that the tertiary sector has now become the engine of development and change, in effect taking the central role allegedly played by manufacturing in the nineteenth century. This necessarily raises the question of whether the services sector has a distinct identity? What precisely is a service?

The conventional view is that services are economic activities which do not have physical output. The whimsical idea that a service is something you cannot drop on your foot is seen by many to encapsulate what we are trying to identify. The output of a service is consumed at the moment it is produced. It supposedly cannot be stored, transported or resold. A haircut, a meal in a restaurant, the repair of washing machine or car, a case dealt with by a doctor or social worker, the processing of a cheque – all are examples of services.

In practice, however, this distinction is nothing like as clear-cut as would first appear. Many services have a physical output: a legal document from a solicitor, a statement of account from a bank, a case analysis produced by a social worker. A meal in a restaurant must be consumed within a short period of time, but it may nonetheless function as a store of value in the sense of a favour done for a business colleague – a favour which antici-pates a return. A holiday may be offered as a prize in a competition along-side a microwave oven or a motor car. In this respect the holiday is different from the other prizes (products) only in that its physical presence is much harder to pin down. In fact the distinction between secondary and tertiary sectors may have more to do with statistical conventions than with essential differences. That is to say, the separate existence of a services sec-tor is in part the result of the need to find a category for economic activities which are difficult to slot into manufacturing. In this sense 'services' is something of a residual category. In fact it is rather like the term 'middle class' under which a wide range of occupations have been traditionally grouped but whose only common characteristic is that they are not 'manual'. Similarly all economic activities which are not unequivocally manufacturing (or agricultural/extractive), although often differing appreciably from each other, are lumped into the single category of 'services'.

The comparison with the term 'middle class' has a parallel in reality in that services are often equated with white-collar occupations. However, the blue-collar/white-collar distinction does not help us as a significant proportion of jobs in the tertiary sector – from driving buses to cleaning hotel bedrooms, from repairing TV sets to serving up fast food – are unquestionably manual. It is certainly true that white-collar workers now make up a majority in industrial society (in Britain in 1981 51 per cent of the labour force), but a significant proportion of these white-collar workers are servicing *manufacturing* as clerks, managers, accountants, industrial designers, draughtsmen and so forth. Conversely it has been estimated that at least 40 per cent of the labour force in the services sector is manual.

Apart from the difficulty of identifying unequivocally a services sector, the notion of a 'march through the sectors', the idea that developed societies have moved through a series of stages in which first the primary, then the secondary, and now the tertiary becomes the dynamic sector – this idea is regarded with scepticism by a number of economic historians. First, we need to remember that a substantial services sector existed before the Industrial Revolution. In fact without a developed banking and insurance network the industrial system could never have taken off. Second, it is doubtful whether in the case of most industrial societies there was ever a phase when industrial workers formed a majority of the labour force. In Britain, it is true that there was a period during the second half of the nineteenth century when this was the case, but Britain in this and other respects is exceptional. In other industrial economies the proportion in agriculture and services combined always outweighed those in manufacturing. In most DCs the industrial core of the economy has stabilised at about one-third of the labour force, with this percentage remaining roughly the same throughout this century. Commenting on these sectoral shifts, sociologist Krishan Kumar concedes that in Britain the industrial labour force has declined more sharply than elsewhere but maintains that this is because it had reached an abnormally high level there in the first place. In France, Germany and the United States the decline has been much less dramatic. So far as Kumar is concerned the most significant change over the past hundred years has been the shift from *agriculture into services*.

'Services', then, is a difficult category. Therefore, in order to assist our understanding of the issues it might be helpful to try to distinguish between types of services. We may identify, first of all, *business services,* the most obvious being transportation, wholesaling and retailing. Banking, insurance, accounting, administrative, professional and technical services should be added to this list. Second, we encounter *public services* in the form of law and order, health, welfare, educational and municipal services. Third, we have *personal services* which can be subdivided into domestic, artisan and professional. Domestic services are cooking, cleaning, gardening, basic repairs and the like; artisan are services provided by skilled workers such as plumbers, motor mechanics and carpenters; and professional personal services refer to those of doctors, solicitors, architects and so forth. Last of all we may identify *entertainment and leisure services* in the form of TV, cinemas, theatres, leisure centres, theme parks and holidays. Having identified these types of services it will be useful to consider briefly why they have expanded (or in some cases contracted) over the past century.

So far as *business services* are concerned these have grown alongside manufacturing. The greater the volume of goods that are produced and traded, the greater the demand for finance, insurance, transportation, wholesale and retail outlets. Furthermore, as the scale of production expanded and firms became organisationally more complex, so the demand for managers, accountants, lawyers and other business professionals increased. During the boom period of capitalism many of these functions were expanded in-house as departments and branches of the large corporations. But the onset of recession and the need for greater economy has led to the off-loading of many of these activities to independent firms.

Public services have on the whole been provided by the state and initially expanded gradually with the growth of urban populations and the acceptance by the state of an increasingly interventionist role. However, the emergence of welfare capitalism during the post-Second World War era saw a significant expansion in administrative, education, health and welfare services – more civil servants, doctors, nurses, teachers and social workers. (Between 1959 and 1981 employment in health and education in Britain expanded by 99 per cent, and in welfare services by 160 per cent.)

So far as *personal services* are concerned the situation is more complex. The demand for personal domestic services is increasingly catered for by consumer durables such as washing-machines, vacuum cleaners and microwaves which are replacing human labour. In this sense employment in personal domestic services has declined. On the other hand, the demand for artisan personal services has grown with the ownership of property and goods (more houses, washing-machines, TVs and fridges to be repaired and maintained). Likewise the demand for personal professional services has expanded with the ownership of property and goods which must be conveyed, financed and insured. Last, to the extent that incomes have grown, more has become available to spend on leisure and entertainment.

So far we have been talking mainly about the expansion in *demand* for services, which does not necessarily mean that they will be supplied. For them to be provided the appropriate technological means must be available but this alone is not enough. Ultimately what decides whether services are *marketed* is, of course, whether a profit can be made from their provision. The issue of profit is vital to the understanding of the market provision of both *goods and services* in capitalist societies. In this light the growth in the private provision of services over the past 25 years or so is to be explained primarily in terms of its being more profitable than manufacturing and hence more attractive in terms of investment opportunities. We need to bear in mind here that labour costs in manufacturing in DCs have risen to a level which makes it increasingly less able to compete with the products of this sector in third world countries. For example, if we take labour costs in Britain in 1981 as 100, the figure for the United States was 117, but for Brazil it was 23, for the Philippines, 10, and for Indonesia, 6. Although these are overall labour costs it is certainly the case that in the services sector in DCs labour has been and is substantially cheaper. This is mainly because of much lower levels of unionisation and the predominance in many areas of female and part-time labour. It is thus no accident that large corporations, MNCs and conglomerates have over the past two decades been diversifying into services, especially hotels and catering, leisure, the holiday industry and financial services. The advent of information technology has vastly increased the power and influence of large corporations in the communications field. It has been estimated that at the end of the eighties 80 large corporations controlled 75 per cent of the international communications market. On one national Philippine TV network channel, nine out of ten large sponsors are MNCs such as Pepsi-Cola, Colgate and Nestlé.

The supremacy of the profit motive has placed a premium on efficiency which means that the provision of services, just as that of manufactured goods, is increasingly subjected to the processes of bureaucratisation and centralisation. Services have, in short, been *industrialised*. This suggests that the post-industrial scenario of meaningful work in pleasant surroundings must be treated with caution. For a start, the services sector contains a good number of contemporary society's lowest-paid and most insalubrious occupations such as those in catering, cleaning, transport and municipal services. But in addition, as we saw in the previous chapter, white-collar, professional and even managerial occupations are more and more subject to loss of autonomy and deskilling under the relentless drive for greater efficiency. Knowledge, we need to bear in mind, is a commodity just like iron, steel, oil, capital equipment or finished goods. Knowledge is not some free-floating entity outside and independent of social institutions as the post-industrial thesis seems to imply. Knowledge must be transmitted through institutions – universities, research institutes, governments, defence establishments and corporations – and is in the process appropriated by these institutions. In a society where the means of production and the commodities they produce are owned privately and must be paid for, so also is the case with knowledge. Even ostensibly public bodies such as universities and research institutes must adapt to the logic of the market in the sense that the knowledge they produce must be relevant to the needs of a society which is dominated by private ownership and the pursuit of profit.

If the expansion of the services sector has been largely determined by market forces then presumably this may work in reverse, that is, demand for services may contract. Such a situation has been most apparent in the case of Britain where in 1981 *public* services accounted for around 38 per cent of total services employment. However the Conservative Government's drive to 'roll back the state' and the cuts in public expenditure this entailed had reduced this figure by almost 10 per cent by the end of the eighties. To some extent the reduction of public services employment in Britain was offset by a rapid growth in financial and other business services, overwhelmingly in the private sector. But this growth was to a considerable extent engendered by a conscious economic policy of removing most of the restraints on credit which among other things produced a spectacular property boom. With the collapse of the property boom at the end of the eighties the future expansion of the services sector seemed in question. In fact in early 1991 the Conservative Government found itself having to concede that the growth in services had probably reached its peak as well as having to recognise that any future expansion in this sector would be tied to a parallel *growth in manufacturing*.

The British economy undoubtedly differs from most of its European counterparts in a least one vital respect: the peculiar economic predominance there of the housing market. Nonetheless this example serves to expose yet another weakness in the post-industrial scenario: that the services sector is set fair to expand continually and that this expansion is quite independent of the secondary sector.

It thus seems more useful to view the growth and contraction of services in the light of market forces (both national and international) rather than in terms of some metaphysical logic of industrialism or axial principle.

Furthermore, in that the production of services seems to be governed by the same processes of centralisation and rationalisation that predominate in manufacturing, then the character of contemporary developed societies remains overwhelmingly *industrial*. For the conceivable future the core activity of the industrial capitalist system will remain the production of material goods.

THE DRIVE FOR A FLEXIBLE LABOUR FORCE

Having emphasised the all-pervading influence of market forces, there can be little doubt that the intense competition that has become the hallmark of the world capitalist system has enormously increased the pressure to reduce the costs of production. This pressure, most commentators would agree, currently expresses itself in a drive for greater flexibility in the conditions under which goods and services are produced. One obvious source of flexibility lies in the conditions under which human labour is utilised in the workplace. First, employees can be required to undertake a wide range of tasks rather than one narrowly demarcated work role. Movement in this direction has been assisted by developments in computer technology which often release the operative from strict routine, thereby permitting significant expansion in the scope of work. For example, the computer technology at Nissan's car factory in the north-east of England no longer requires that the operative be tied to the assembly line, leaving him/her free to develop technical, design and other specialised skills – in fact a situation predicted by Blauner in the late fifties and one very much in line with the post-industrial scenario. However, before we conclude that flexibility neatly fits both the needs of employers and employees, we need to be aware that it (flexibility) expresses itself in other ways. Most obviously this can be seen in the character of the actual conditions under which labour is employed.

A major problem for all employers is that of matching the size of one's labour force with the demand for one's product. When demand is slack it would be very convenient were employers able to reduce their labour force accordingly. To some extent this has always happened. However, complete freedom of action here has in the past been circumscribed by legal impediments such as strictures on redundancy and unfair dismissal backed ultimately by the power of the trade unions. However, the 1980s saw a significant diminution of trade union power primarily because the heartland of trade union membership in industrial societies, manufacturing and the public sector, both contracted significantly. Manufacturing was hard hit by the relocation of jobs in this sector to other areas of the world, particularly newly industrialised countries (see Box 2.1). And second, the public sector has had to bear the weight of a series of cutbacks with the abandonment of Keynesian economics in the face of world recession. The unemployment engendered by the decline of both sectors, as well as by technological change, has further weakened the bargaining power of trade unions and generally undermined the ability of labour (both organised and unorganised) to resist the drive for greater flexibility. This flexibility can manifest itself at this level in a variety of ways: greater powers of hiring and firing, the imposition of short-term contracts, subcontracting, including requiring former employees to become self-employed (very evident in the British building industry in the latter part of the eighties for example), together with a range of other devices which have decisively shifted the balance of power in favour of employers. It should be pointed out, in addition, that insofar as any expansion in the labour force has taken place over the past decade this has been in the services sector. The service sector, we note, is particularly associated with flexible labour conditions, conditions made possible by low levels of unionisation and high rates of part-time labour – much of it female. (Part-time labour is not usually covered by employment legislation.)

In the light of the drive for a flexible labour force which is evident in all contemporary industrial societies, commentators have proposed, as we approach the end of this century, two basic types of worker. First, a *core* labour force working mainly for large corporations enjoying more or less permanent employment with relatively high salaries, good working conditions and fringe benefits such as access to cheap loans and free medical insurance. These fringe benefits, which could also include sports and recreational facilities, are part of a total package aimed at strengthening identity with the company and its products. Such companies, whether in manufacturing or services, will tend to be non-unionised but will have staff associations whose primary function will be to serve as a conduit for company policy. In return for these benefits core employees will accept flexible work roles, being prepared to perform a number of work tasks, cover for absent colleagues, retrain and perhaps be geographically mobile. The emphasis will be on the employee's accepting greater responsibility for the product of his/her labour. This may manifest itself in various forms of participation, Quality Circles and the like. Enhancement of responsibility serves the dual functions of being in line with the job enrichment movement whilst at the same time strengthening identity with management.

The *peripheral* labour force, by contrast, will endure unstable conditions of employment, a generally poor working environment and low pay. Many of its members will be short-term or part-time employees often working and unsocial hours. Females and members of ethnic minorities will be over-represented in this peripheral labour force. Whether peripherals will continue to constitute a minority (albeit a sizeable minority), as appeared to be the case at the beginning of the nineties, is extremely difficult to determine. Were they to become a majority, what would be the social and political implications? Such questions we must leave until the concluding chapter of this book. In the meantime it is necessary to comment on the influence in Europe of the Japanese model of management, not least because it bears upon most of the issues discussed in this and the two previous chapters, including that of a core/peripheral labour force.

JAPANISATION

As we have seen, Japan passed through a very different pattern of industrialisation and modernisation to that of Europe and the United States. The rapidity of social and economic change in Japan has meant that many aspects of the feudal era have survived into the twentieth century. This is most apparent in Japan's strong collectivist ethic which manifests itself in a deep attachment to group whether this be the family, school or firm. It seems to be the case that in Japan the group has primacy over the individual. Japanese-American specialist William Ouchi, for example, informs us that individually based incentive schemes do not work in the Japanese environment since the Japanese are unwilling to take personal credit for what they see as group outcomes.

A central role in Japan's astonishing economic revival has been imputed to the Japanese corporation and to Japanese management style. Three characteristics of Japan's corporate system are highlighted to explain this success. First, there is the lifelong employment offered by the large corporations. Every year the corporations recruit a pool of new employees direct from schools and universities, irrespective of whether there are, in the immediate term, specific jobs for the new recruits. Thereafter the new entrant will remain with the firm for the rest of *his* (virtually no females are employed on this basis) working life. He will be promoted at regular intervals irrespective of individual job performance. Dismissal is a very rare phenomenon and would require a very serious, usually criminal offence. The second feature is that Japanese corporations lack the specialised career paths of Euro-American system. Employees are trained in all aspects of their level of work and are expected to slot in at several points in the organisation. This absence of rigid specialisation makes possible highly flexible organisational structures. And third, the group in the Japanese corporation predominates over the individual; collective consensus over individual needs and ambitions. This ethos is a reflection of Japanese culture in general with its Confucian emphasis on the collectivity. According to Ouchi, 'In the Japanese mind, collectivism is neither a corporate nor individual goal to strive for, nor a slogan to pursue. Rather the nature of things operates so that nothing of consequence occurs as a result of individual effort. Everything important in life happens as a result of teamwork or collective effort. Therefore to attempt to assign individual credit or blame to results is unfounded' ('Japanese Management: The Art of Self-Regulation' in G. Morgan (1939) *Creative Organisation*, Sage). (Now see Box 8.2.)

A particularly important consequence of this group ethos is that the deep-rooted suspicion and lack of trust which has characterised British and to some extent European labour – management relations is largely absent from Japan. Japanese trade unions, for example, invariably identify strongly with their corporation and its management. Each large corporation has its own trade union which will see its role as that of promoting management policy. This will include monitoring worker performance and

---

Box 8.2 Theory Z

On the basis of the Japanese experience Ouchi purposed that American companies adopt a Theory Z type of environment. The term Theory Z is a conscious allusion to D. McGregor's Theory Y, aiming to develop it further by using the insights derived from Ouchi's study of Japanese corporations. A Theory Z environment would include:

● Long-term employment, often for a lifetime
● Relatively slow process of evaluation and promotion
● Non-specialised career paths
● Mainly informal mechanisms of control
● Collective decision-making
● Collective responsibility
● Broad concern for the general welfare of subordinates and co-workers

Ouchi suggests that a good deal of movement in this direction has already taken place in a few large American corporations: IBM, Procter and Gamble and Eastman–Kodak are given as examples. In Britain Marks and Spencer have been claimed to subscribe to a Theory Z type of culture.

Sources: William Ouchi (1981) *Theory Z: How American Business Can Meet its Japanese Challenges*, Reading, Mass., Addison-Wesley; Michio Morishima (1982) *Why Has Japan Succeeded*, Cambridge University Press.

disciplining those who do not come up to the mark. Indeed it is not unusual for union officials to engage in the harassment and victimisation of workers who do not conform to company norms and practices. It is important to appreciate that the Japanese unions did go through a militant period after the Second World War. However, during a series of highly confrontational strikes in the fifties the independent power of the unions was broken as a result of a coordinated and determined effort by the employers.

In fact Japanese corporations are not quite as harmonious as some Western enthusiasts seem to think. If we look behind appearances it seems that the collectivist ethic is strongly reinforced from above. Accordingly the much-vaunted Quality Circles are not always as voluntary as their protagonists would claim. At Matsushita, for example, voluntary activity in a Quality Circle amounts to contributing suggestions – three a month – which are ranged by supervisors on a scale, one to nine. Such contributions will form part of regular appraisal which will affect earnings and promotion prospects. Generally speaking, employees who exhibit inadequate levels of commitment to the corporations's goals will encounter various forms of pressure, both subtle and not so subtle.

But perhaps the most serious disincentive to challenging the collectivism of the Japanese corporation is the employees' dependence on it. With the large corporations offering housing loans, medical insurance, pensions and other critical fringe benefits, the employee is tied whether he likes it or not. The lifetime employment principle means that mobility between corporations for both management and labour has until recently been virtually non-existent. Since the corporations recruit directly from school or university there is no other means of access. More important, lifetime employment is a much-prized possession, being available only to a minority of Japanese adults. Females for a start are excluded and of males probably less than 40 per cent obtain this prize. The remainder of the labour force work for small firms where wages are appreciably lower, working conditions often poor and fringe benefits largely unavailable. Many of these small firms are locked into subcontracting arrangements with the corporate giants.

There has been a good deal of debate as to whether the Japanese approach to management can be transferred, lock, stock and barrel, to the European context. Sceptics have highlighted Europe's strong tradition of individualism which contrasts markedly with Japanese collectivism. Added to this is Europe's long history of independent trade unions and, overall, a more confrontational 'low trust' approach to industrial relations. However, with the decline in trade union power over the past decade and the high levels of unemployment which both lie behind and express it, a major obstacle has been significantly reduced in size. It is not at all insignificant that where Japanese employment practices have been introduced into Britain, usually with negligible resistance, it has been in areas of high unemployment such as West Lothian and Tyneside (30 per cent). In fact when Nissan started up its famous factory in Sunderland an advertisement for 500 jobs attracted 11 500 applications. This highlights the fact that the acceptability of a given set of working arrangements is in no small measure related to the state of the labour market. Ironically, the reverse situation seems to be developing in Japan where a serious shortage of labour is enabling employees increasingly to resist the very working practices that their counterparts in depressed areas of Europe are accepting. At the beginning of 1992 it was estimated that there were in Japan roughly twice as many new jobs on offer as there were applicants to fill them. In such a job market employees were able to demand less overtime, shorter hours and longer holidays, thereby suggesting that the Japanese are not the workaholics they have been made out to be in the West. Furthermore, a shortage of talent has not only enabled employees to 'job-hop' from corporation to corporation, but has forced senior management to rush high-fliers up the hierarchy. This latter, of course, constitutes a radical break with the long-established tradition of promotion and salaries being closely linked to seniority. Such was the degree of change sweeping through the Japanese corporate system during the early nineties that one economist was led to speculate that the system of lifetime employment would eventually be destroyed.

Whether this prediction will be borne out by future events is at this stage impossible to say. However, it and the changes that lie behind it warn us against taking a static view of Japanese society, assuming it to be set in a rigid and unchanging mould. What seems to be taking place is a convergence between the Western and Japanese forms of work organisation. Underlying this convergence is the ever closer integration of the world economy and the ratcheting up of competition which this produces. The intensification of competition expresses itself in a variety of ways but not least in steadily increasing pressure to peripheralise an expanding section of the labour force.

Thus 'Japanisation' is something of a blanket term, a convenient masthead under which are assembled a range of techniques and policies of varying pedigree. Many of these techniques have their origins in the long-standing Euro-American experience of management efforts to win over the labour force, whether through nineteenth-century paternalism, industrial psychology, Human Relations, job enrichment or other incentive programmes. Whatever the current concoction it is best understood as part of the unending quest for an industrial culture: an integral constellation of

norms, values and symbols, which will harness the energies and commitment of the labour force to the ebb and flow of the market.

CONCLUSION

In this chapter the notion of a *post*-industrial society has been criticised on
a number of grounds. These criticisms centre on two basic themes in the
post-industrial scenario: the first is that advanced industrial economies
have entered a phase of development in which services have become the
leading sector, the seat of innovation and growth. And, second, following
on from this is that the character of work in this post-industrial society is
being transformed into non-alienated knowledge production in generally
congenial non-bureaucratised surroundings.

So far as the first point is concerned it is certainly true that the services
sector (recognising the difficulties of pinning it down) has assumed a much
greater preponderance in advanced economies than was the case half a century ago. However, rather than interpreting this apparent transformation in
terms of the outworkings of some underlying scientific logic, it has been
suggested that it is better explained in the light of a long-term restructuring
of the world economy. The expansion of services is indissolubly linked to
the decline of manufacturing; in effect both processes are different sides of
the same coin. The decline of manufacturing in both Europe and the United
States is explained primarily by its falling profitability and consequent
relocation to other areas of the globe such as newly industrialising countries and various sites in the third world. Correspondingly, the expansion of
services should be understood mainly as offering alternative areas of
investment and profitability. The greater profitability of services over manufacturing in developed economies arises principally from cheaper labour
costs, services typically having access to a more flexible workforce than
the more traditional unionised labour of manufacturing. The (usually invol-
untary) flexibility of the labour force in many areas of the services sector
must lead us to question the second main assumption of the post-industrial
thesis which proposes an overall improvement in working conditions. On
the contrary, the increasing pressure for more subcontracting, short-term,
part-time and other forms of flexible employment conditions in *all* areas of
advanced economies, raises the question not just of working conditions but
of the future of work as traditionally conceived itself. However, to this fundamental question we shall return in our final chapter. In the meantime we
may conclude this chapter by observing that available evidence would
seem to indicate that the industrial landscape of the immediate future will

continue to be dominated by large, usually multinational, corporations. These corporations will be operated by a core and relatively privileged labour force buffered by large numbers of peripherals, many of them women who can be dispensed with during periods of falling demand. Closely tied to these large units through subcontracting agreements of varying degrees of stringency will be a range of small firms supplying components, specialised lines or services. Many of these small firms will approximate to the family-based artisan workshops of the pre-industrial period, except, of course, that they will have a high-tech base.

BIBLIOGRAPHY

Allen, J. and Massey, D. (eds) (1988) *The Economy in Question* (London: Sage).
Butler, S. (1992) 'Looking West for Inspiration', *Financial Times*, 24 February 1992.
Galbraith, J. K. (1967) *The New Industrial State* (Hamondsworth: Penguin).
Hartwell, R. M. (1973) 'The Service Revolution', in C. M. Cipolla (ed.), *The Industrial Revolution* (London: Fontana).
Kumar, K. (1978) *Prophecy and Progress* (London: Allen Lane).
Lyon, D. (1988) *The Information Society* (Oxford: Polity Press).
Stanworth, C. (1991) 'Japanese Management Development and its Application in Britain', *Future of Work Research Group Brief,* No. 32, Polytechnic of Central London.
Stanworth, C. (1992) 'Japanese Working Practices and Japanisation in the UK', *Future of Work Research Group Brief,* No. 33, Polytechnic of Central London.

9 Concluding Remarks: Beyond Capitalism?

The basic focus of this book has been upon industrialisation and the emergence of industrial society. It will be apparent by now that industrialisation is an ongoing process, indeed that the 'industrial revolution' continues to unfold as we move into the twenty-first century. The technological and social upheavals of the eighteenth century eventually produced a society that was radically different from anything that had previously existed in human history. Without repeating the core differences outlined at the end of Chapter 3, it is worth highlighting two of the most fundamental at this point. First, industrial society is the first in human history in which an overwhelming majority of the population came to be concentrated in towns and cities. This concentration in urban areas as well as in large units of production created major problems of integration for the new society. How was this huge and potentially volatile mass of people to be contained? The problem was exacerbated during the early stages of industrialisation by the highly unfavourable conditions in which large numbers of people were constrained to live. However, the gradual improvement of living standards as the twentieth century unrolled progressively eased the problem of integration as successive waves of the working class were incorporated into the new society. Eventually the attainment of the stage of high mass consumption in Europe after the Second World War, together with the consolidation of welfare capitalism, seemed to many to have finally solved the problem of material scarcity as well as the social instability it invariably produced. Here we encounter the second fundamental feature of industrial capitalist society: its ability to produce stupendously high living standards for most of its citizens. By the end of the fifties (more than three decades behind North Americans) Western Europeans were benefiting from levels of living on a scale that would have been inconceivable a mere twenty years earlier. Furthermore, it was the vastly enhanced productive capacity of these economies that permitted a surplus to be creamed off (through taxation) and used to establish comprehensive welfare and social security systems. But whilst vastly improved living standards and the spread of mass democracy undoubtedly reduced deep-rooted and pervasive social strains, tension and discontent continued to manifest themselves in specific areas, not least the workplace. The Fordist solution, which permitted these high levels of affluence, depended partly on the diffusion of mass production methods in order to achieve the economies of scale that were needed to produce the cheap consumer durables which both underpinned and expressed the 'age of affluence'. However, such methods of work organisation seem universally to be associated with industrial pathologies such as low levels of job satisfaction, casual absenteeism, sabotage, theft and workplace conflict generally. Whilst by no means all forms of work in industrial societies are organised on a mass-production basis, the pressures of rationalisation and bureaucratisation seem to have been sufficiently strong and pervasive to stimulate widespread concern about the 'quality of working life'. Accordingly the seventies saw increasing interest on the part of employers and governments in the rehumanisation of work through various forms of job enrichment, job redesign, the introduction of Quality Circles and more participatory approaches to management.

However, such efforts as were made to improve the quality of working life have to some extent been overtaken by the world recession of the eighties and the concerted effort to drive down the price of labour that has been one of its principal consequences. The quest for more flexible conditions of employment could mean that employees benefiting from enrichment programmes belong to a minority 'core' labour force, with the majority enduring unfavourable and unstable working conditions. There seems to be little doubt that temporary, casual, part-time and various forms of subcontracted employment are an increasingly important feature of advanced industrial economies. But even the drive for flexibility is now overshadowed by the growing crisis within Fordism. As we saw in Chapter 7 Fordism embodies the notion of relatively high wages permitting high levels of consumption of goods and services, thereby creating further employment at high wages and so on. But everywhere it has been institutionalised, Fordism has had to be buttressed by high levels of state expenditure to maintain adequate levels of employment. In the United States this took the form mainly of high rates of defence spending which had huge spin-offs in terms of contracts and employment. In Europe Fordism was supported by Keynesian policies of full employment together with the widespread distribution of social and welfare benefits.

The Fordist solution has proved increasingly unworkable for basically three reasons. First, manufacturing employment in DCs has been steadily draining away over a long period to low-labour-cost LDCs. Second, the decline of manufacturing employment was to some extent offset by the growth in services but here the public sector played a significant role. But with the onset of recession in the eighties and the adoption of monetarism, the public sector has been subjected to serious pruning, thereby reducing appreciably its employment capacity. And, third, these two factors have been complemented by general technological advance, especially the microchip revolution which is increasingly replacing human beings by machines in all areas of economic activity, services as well as manufacturing. 'Jobless growth' is a term used more and more frequently to denote the process under which Western economies continue to expand but without creating new jobs. Indeed, for some, the long-term view is that the number of jobs is contracting, although the rate at which this is happening is a matter of some dispute.

These and other factors have combined not only to conjure up, yet again, the spectre of mass unemployment, but to raise the question of the future of work itself. That is, to what extent can the norm of a full-time lifetime job at good rates of pay be sustained on a mass scale? A considerable body of informed opinion from sociologists, futurologists, journalists and the like strongly suggests that it cannot. Accordingly a good deal of attention has been devoted to the problem of how a dwindling stock of work can be shared around. A shorter working week, job-sharing, mid-career sabbaticals, early retirement and the raising of the school leaving age are among the more prominent proposals. Whether these singly or in combination will substantially alleviate the problem is an extremely complex question which is quite outside the scope of this book. The point is that so far as politicians and policy-makers are concerned minimal attention has been paid to this problem, particularly in Britain. That is to say, there is still a strong public commitment on the part of politicians of most political persuasions to the belief that enough lifetime work can be made available so long as the *right* economic policies are adopted. Very few public figures (including trade unionists) have been prepared to stand up and concede that we should give up the idea of jobs for all and concentrate on searching for policies which will permit the 'workless' to avail themselves of the benefits of civil society. On the contrary, unemployment is currently viewed as a necessary by-product of industrial efficiency, the price we must pay for remaining competitive. In fact unemployment is frequently blamed on the unemployed themselves who are supposed to have unrealistically high expectations about wages, are feckless, spongers and so on.

In the meantime, in a society where we are continually bombarded by images which insist that we should be consuming more and more, an increasing proportion of our fellow citizens are being denied the means to indulge in the cult of unending self-gratification. It now seems certain that the social disruption produced be the long-term decline in employment has been severely exacerbated by the economic policies pursued particularly in Britain and the United States during the eighties. Between 1979 and 1987 average income in Britain rose by 23 per cent, but for the poorest tenth of the population the rise was a negligible 0.1 per cent. Over the same period the better-off half of the population increased its share of total income from 68 to 73 per cent whilst the poorer sections of society saw their share fall for the first time since 1945. In the United States a decade of economic expansion during the eighties failed to improve the poverty rate which at 12.8 per cent amounted to one in eight Americans living in poverty. More disturbing is the fact that the US poverty rate for blacks is about 30 per cent and for black children 40 per cent. In 1988 the median income for whites was roughly twice that for blacks, but the disparity in *wealth* was much greater, with white households typically ten times more wealthy that their black counterparts. These data suggest that even were black incomes to catch up, major disparities would persist because of accumulated differences in wealth (that is, investments and ownership of property). It is worth pointing out at this point that all industrial capitalist societies contain sizeable communities of ethnic minorities. So far as Western Europe is concerned these owe their existence primarily to a tide of immigration in the fifties and sixties which was fuelled by the postwar boom and the demand for cheap labour that it created. The evidence from Britain and other European countries is that (with some exceptions) non-whites are over-represented in unskilled manual occupations, the unemployed and those living in poverty generally.

Since the Industrial Revolution the idea that work and working hard should be a central life activity has been continually reaffirmed through a succession of social institutions – family, school, the mass media and the wider culture. Work – what you do for a living – has been and remains the principal mechanism through which industrial society allocates its rewards, both material and social. In the light of this paramountcy of work, the fact that those without it not only have a lower status but are also denied access to most of the fruits which industrial society produces is an obvious source of tension. To the extent that the absence of work, and the social exclusion which flows from it, becomes a condition permanent enough to permit the formation of an underclass, the social cohesion of industrial society will be seriously undermined. The fact that a disproportionate number of this emerging underclass may be drawn from ethic minorities for whom material deprivation is augmented by social exclusion will obviously amplify the disadvantages experienced by its members.

In these concluding remarks so far we have noted some of the major contradictions within the capitalist industrial societies (contradictions which the post-industrialists have tended to ignore as did the Industrial Society theorists before them). By 'contradictions' we mean the negative consequences that have arisen out of the activity of producing enormous quantities of goods and services, consequences which, were they to intensify, could undermine the productive system itself. The negative consequences for the quality of working life that followed the dissemination of methods of mass production is one such contradiction. Growing inequality and the emergence of an underclass is a second.

A third major contradiction lies in the obviously negative consequences for the environment of a system which, first, gobbles up the earth's natural resources – fossil fuels, trees, water, mineral ores – at a truly alarming rate and, second, whose factories, power stations and households pollute the atmosphere and dump various forms of waste into rivers, oceans or holes in the ground on such a scale as to constitute a threat to health and even life (both animal and human) itself. Western civilization's dilemma in this respect is encapsulated in the motor car, from most angles the embodiment of twentieth-century material progress; the heart of the Fordist system; a core symbol of achievement and power. Every year the number of cars on the road grows on average by more than the amount it grew the previous year. This not only uses up more steel, chrome, rubber, glass, plastic and petrol, but releases ever-increasing quantities of carbon dioxide and sulphur dioxide into the atmosphere as well as clogging up our towns and cities (not to mention killing and maiming hundreds of thousands of people every year in road accidents – 5 000 deaths per year in Britain alone). It cannot be denied that industrial civilisation, in reducing humankind's dependence upon and subjection to the arbitrariness of nature, has been a truly liberating force. But if in the process that natural world is denuded, impoverished, plundered to a degree that makes it barely habitable, then liberation will be degraded into new forms of bondage. The mediaeval peasant was wholly dependent upon and powerless before the natural forces which seemed to conspire to make his life impossible. The citizen of advanced capitalist societies, by contrast, is driven by material needs, the satisfaction of which could transform living in urban industrial society into an 'air-conditioned nightmare'.

However, when all is said and done, environmental issues are problems mainly for the fortunate minority who inhabit the developed world. For those living in the third world the more pressing concern of meeting one's basic needs has much greater urgency. The peasant farmers of Guatemala, Burkina Faso or Bangladesh, the petty traders of Rio, Lagos or Bombay are daily absorbed with feeding their families with little time to concern themselves about polluted rivers or disappearing forests. And here we encounter what is undoubtedly the most deep-rooted and serious contradiction which afflicts the industrial capitalist system: throughout this book the global character of capitalism has been a basic theme. With the flowering of mercantile capitalism from the sixteenth century on, the expansion of the system has depended upon the successive incorporation of different areas of the world to the extent that there can now be very few spots remote enough to be untouched by it. This means that peoples all over the world – nomads, forest dwellers, fishermen, peasant farmers, urban artisans – are to varying degrees brought face to face with 'modernity' in the form of the industrial system and what it produces. The Fulani nomads of northern Nigeria can still be seen herding their cattle according to a regime which has changed relatively little for centuries. But many of them now carry huge ghetto-blasters on which they listen to Western pop music interspersed by adverts for soap powder, lager beer and chocolate biscuits. The peasant farmers of highland Peru and southern India gather nightly around the village TV set to watch soap operas, Euro-American sitcoms and game shows as well as out-of-date Schwarzenegger films. Smart young men and women in Los Angeles, Milan, Singapore and Manila wear the same jeans and trainers (although those worn by the Los Angelinos and Milanese are now probably made in Singapore and Manila). However, apart from an expanding but still by Western standards small middle class, the majority of the inhabitants of the third world are ill-placed to acquire more than a pathetic handful from the treasure house of consumer goods that is paraded before them. It seems that the second contradiction mentioned above – growing inequality within advanced capitalist societies – is replicated at a global level but in much starker terms. We cannot fail to be aware of the staggeringly wide gap in overall living standards between rich and poor countries, a gap which, according to a number of sources, is growing steadily wider. How and whether this fundamental contradiction will express itself in the form of serious social conflict both within and across national borders is extremely difficult to predict. What seems certain is that the negative consequences of this and other contradictions discussed are unlikely to be contained – insofar as it will be possible to contain them – without extensive state intervention in the market. The establishment of huge trading blocks sheltering from each other behind tariff walls comprising groups of (core) developed states linked to specific (peripheral) less-developed countries through ties of economic interest looks increasingly feasible. And at the national level, an administered society presided over by large corporations in partnership with interventionist governments no longer seems the aberration it was thought to be in the eighties. In fact the degree of intervention at all levels may be such that market capitalism will have been superseded by some form of planned 'post-capitalism': a type of high-tech mercantilism. Ironically the programmed and planned social order which the Industrial

Society theorists and post-industrialists envisage may be brought into being by the kind of intense and far-reaching upheavals that their analyses see as largely obsolescent.

BIBLIOGRAPHY

Deem, R. and Salaman, G. (eds) (1985) *Work, Culture and Society* (Milton Keynes: Open University Press).
Handy, C. (1984) *The Future of Work* (Oxford: Blackwell).
Hall, S. Held, D. and McGrew, T. (eds) (1992) *Modernity and its Futures* (Oxford: Polity Press).
Lyon, D. (1988) *The Information Society* (Oxford: Polity Press).
Scase, R. (ed.) (1989) *Industrial Societies* (London: Unwin Hyman).
Veal, A. J. (1987) *Leisure and the Future* (London: Allen & Unwin).

Index

Lyon, D. 143, 150
Macmillan, H. 56
management
  by function 79, 80
  by level 79, 80
  definition of 78–9
  Japanese 124, 138–42
  participative, 122–4
  patrimonial 0, 71
  problems of 45
  science 85
managerial politics 80
managers 53
  activities of 79, 80
  recruitment of 81
manual sector 113, 114
manufacturing sector 128, 130, 131,
  134–6, 142, 144
'march through the sectors' 132
Marshall Aid 58
Marks and Spencer 139
Marx, K. 42
  and alienation 108, 118
  and Engels 48–50, 52, 53, 69
  and the 'new middle class' 54
  and small firms 83
  and social mobility 55
mass democracy 59, 144
mass markets 107
mass production 106, 107, 112, 145
Massey, D. 143
Matsushita 140
Mayo, E. 98–101
McGregor, D. 122
McHugh, D. 126
McLellan, D. 108, 126
mercantilism 149
merchant capital 38
microchip revolution 85, 86, 129, 103
  and small firms 85, 86
middle class 130, 132
  'new middle class' 53–5
Model T. 106
modern society 127
modernisation 46
monetarism 67, 107
monopoly 73
monopoly capitalism 111, 112
Mullins, L. J. 86, 126
multinational corporation (MNCs) 22–5,
  58, 74, 134, 143

National Association of Estate Agents
  115

National Health Service 62
newly industrialising countries (NICs) 25,
  26
'new middle class' 53–5
Nissan, 136, 141

oligopoly 24, 83, 85
Olivetti 121
Ouchi, W. 138
Owen, R. 72

participant observation 8
participation 122, 141, 144
  power-centred 122
  task-centred 123
patrimonialism 70, 71, 76, 77
peasants
  under feudalism 29–31
  peasant agriculture 20, 30, 70, 148
  and proletarianisation 42, 43
peripheral labour force 137, 138, 143
Pollard, S. 73, 86
post-capitalism 149–50
post-Fordism 130
post-industrial society 25
  evaluation of 131–6
  perspective 128–30
Postan, M. M. 47
Principles of Scientific Management
  (Taylor) 94
privatised worker 65, 110
Procter and Gamble 139
professional management 71, 78–80
professionalisation 114, 115
professions 114, 115, 130, 134
proletarianisation 33, 42, 43
proletariat 48, 49
*Protestant Ethic and the Spirit of Capitalism,
  The* (Weber) 41
Pugh, D. S. 77, 105, 126
'putting-out' system 35, 39, 43, 84

Quality Circles 124, 137, 140, 144
Quality of Working Life, The (Department of
  Employment Report) 120
questionnaires 7

Radice, H. 27
Reid, S. 115, 116, 126
reskilling, 113, 114, 125, 130
Rider, J. 69
Rolls-Royce, 124
Rose, M. 105
Rostow, W. W. 27, 69, 107

154

Index